GETTING ALONG

by the
Whale Research Group
Illustrated by Don Wright

©1984 The Whale Research Group, Memorial University of Newfoundland

Canadian Cataloguing in Publication Data

Main entry under title:

Getting along —— fish, whales, and fishermen

For use in elementary schools.
ISBN 0-919519-78-4

1. Marine ecology — Juvenile literature. 2. Marine resources — Newfoundland — Juvenile literature.
3. Whales — Newfoundland — Juvenile literature.
4. Fisheries — Newfoundland — Juvenile literature.
I. Memorial University of Newfoundland, Whale Research Group.

QH541.5.S3G47 1984   574.92'1634   C84-099419-2

CAUTION

No part of this publication may be photocopied, or otherwise reproduced, without the Publisher's permission: Breakwater Books Ltd., 277 Duckworth Street, St. John's, Newfoundland, A1C 1G9.

INTRODUCTION

What Will You Learn?

Are there mountains under the sea?
Where do waves come from?
What is the largest animal ever to live on earth?
Can you fingerprint a whale?
What is a basking shark?
What do fish, whales and fishermen have in common?

This book was prepared to help you answer these and other questions and to show why fish, whales and fishermen need to get along. *Getting Along* was developed by the whale research group of Memorial University, along with some Newfoundland teachers. The whale research group is a group of scientists who study the marine environment of Newfoundland and Labrador and prepare papers, books, posters and talks to help the people of this province better understand the sea life around them.

Getting Along is about our ocean and the plants and animals that live in it. There are eight lessons. You will start studying the ocean and what it's made of. Next you'll learn that every living thing has a special *address*, and job to do in the environment. You'll study examples of *who eats whom* in the sea. By the middle of the book, you'll understand how living organisms depend on one another and together form an environment that is finely balanced. Whales live in the ocean. You'll learn to identify the common whales found around Newfoundland and Labrador and to estimate the size of a whale population. Next you'll learn what extinction means. The book finishes by looking at a resource conflict here in Newfoundland and Labrador, between whales and fishermen. There are no bad guys in this story, just problems to be understood and worked out. Through the knowledge you gain as you go along, you'll see there is a joint solution.

Each lesson has lots of pictures, activities and questions to help you learn. Some of the words used may not be familiar to you and so each lesson ends with a list of new words and definitions. The first time one of these words is used, it has a signal * beside it to show you there is a definition at the end of the lesson.

Getting Along was tried out on grade five students and their teachers before it was completed. We especially thank the students in Newfoundland and Labrador who reviewed it for us. Their comments and suggestions have been passed on to each of you, the new grade five students who will be reading this.

Lesson 1

THE OCEAN

What do you know about the ocean?

Look at a map of the world. You can see countries, continents and oceans.

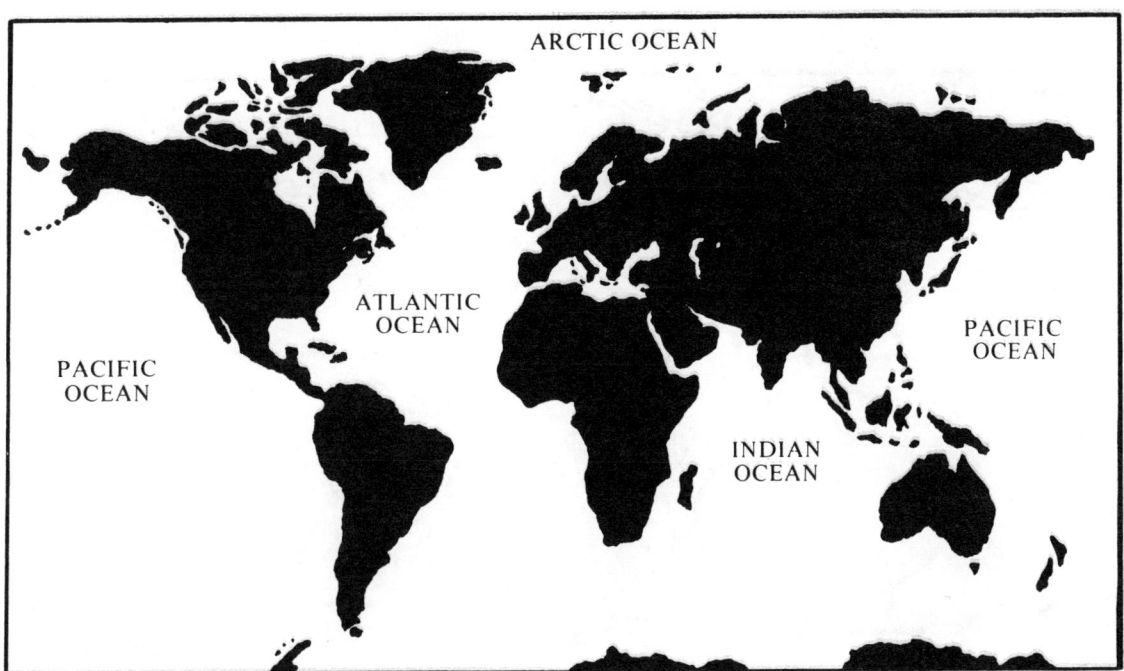

Questions
1. *What are the names of the oceans?*
2. *How many oceans are there?*
3. *Are there several oceans or is there just one?*

Dr. Alex Hay is an *oceanographer** at Memorial University, in St. John's. He says there is only one main ocean. He says that continents like Africa and North America are really only land masses within this one larger ocean. Oceans, seas, gulfs and bays are really just parts of the one world ocean. Do you agree? Look at the world map again.

What do you know about the ocean? You probably know it covers over 70% of the earth's surface. You probably know it contains salt water and many living things. Do you know about ocean *rivers*? about tides? about underwater mountain ranges? There is much to be learned!

Rivers in the Ocean

Ocean waters are always on the move. In some places, water moves with a tremendous force like that of a raging river. Sometimes it just moves up and down. Movements of ocean water are called *currents**.

The temperature of the water and the strength of the wind influence ocean currents. Cold arctic water is slowly replaced by warmer water from the *tropics*, the region around the equator. Winds blowing on both sides of the tropics push the warm water westward. The ocean currents change direction when they come up against the continents. As a result, there are many ocean currents going in many directions.

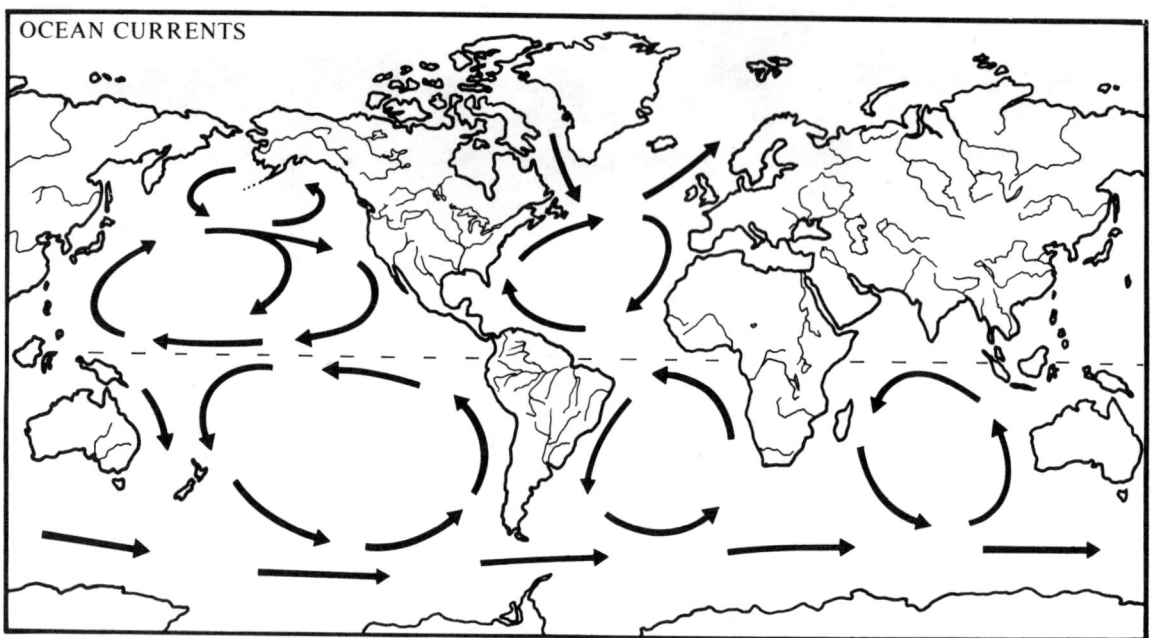

Questions

4. What are the names of the two main ocean currents found around Newfoundland and Labrador?
5. Where does each begin?
6. Where do they meet?
7. Can you think of ways these currents influence the weather in Newfoundland? (Hint: what happens when cold air meets warm air?)

Tides

The daily rise and fall of the ocean water is called the tide. There are usually four tides of different heights each day, two high tides and two low tides. At high tide, the water rises and flows inshore. At low tide, the water recedes or goes down and moves offshore.

Tides are caused by the *gravitational** attraction of the sun and moon for the earth. This gravitational force has a great effect on the water of the earth because water moves easily. When the moon is in line with the sun and they pull together on the earth, the highest tides occur. These are called the *spring tides**. When the moon is at right angles to the sun, the pull of the sun is partially cancelled by the pull of the moon and vice versa, and their effect is not as strong. These tides, called *neap tides** are weaker and there is less difference between high and low tide. The times of the tides and the levels reached by them are influenced by other factors too: the location of the tide, the shape of the ocean bottom in specific places and the currents and winds at specific times. All around the earth, high and low tides occur at different times.

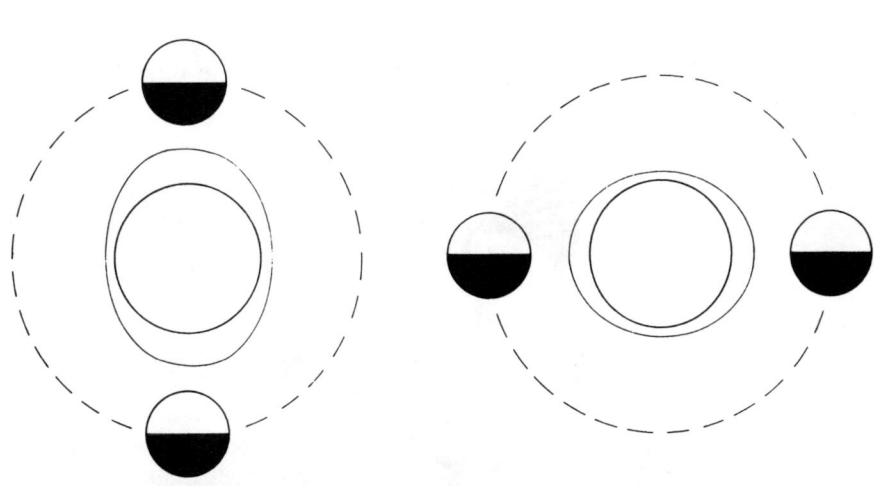

LOW TIDE    HIGH TIDE

- **Some Things To Do**

  If you live near the ocean, go to the shore and place a stick or marker at the highest point the water reaches on the shore while you're there. Check the marker in a few hours. Is the tide rising or falling?

  Check your local paper to see what times high tide and low tide will occur. If you can't find tide information in the paper, call your local radio station.

Questions

8. *Name the phases of the moon when the highest tides occur.*

9. *Why is it important for fishermen to know the times of high and low tide?*

Ocean Waves

Have you ever been seasick? Waves cause seasickness. They also cause changes in beaches and sometimes damage to buildings and boats. We build breakwaters to create protected harbours and help prevent damage due to waves.

Waves are not all bad though! Surfers certainly enjoy them. Waves are also very important to all ocean life because they help move nutrients and oxygen through the water.

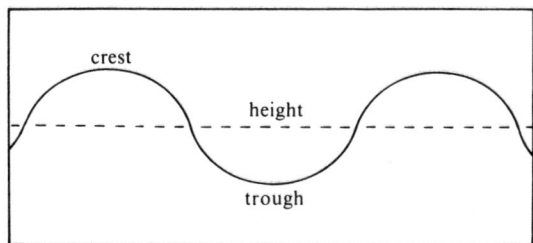

What causes waves? Remember, currents are affected by winds. Winds are also responsible for *ocean waves**. When the wind blows across the surface of the ocean, it pushes the water into waves. Each wave is followed by a hollow. The highest part of a wave is called the *crest* and the lowest part between crests, the hollow, is called the *trough*. The vertical distance between the crest and the trough is the height of a wave.

Waves come in all shapes and sizes. The size of a wave depends on how strongly the wind blows, how long it blows and how far it blows across the water without being slowed down by land.

*Seismic waves** are created by earthquakes or landslides on the ocean floor. Seismic waves are very long and travel at high speeds. They are highly destructive when they reach the shore because they are so big and powerful. In the United States, seismic waves are called *tidal waves* even though they have nothing to do with tides. In Japan, seismic waves are called *tsunami*. This word is being used more and more by oceanographers around the world.

Questions

10. Which marine mammals like to surf by riding on waves caused by the bow wake of ships?
11. During the storm which caused the Ocean Ranger disaster of 1982, a wave was measured. The crest was 14 metres above sea level and the trough was one metre below sea level. What was the height of the wave?

In November 1929, a tidal wave struck Newfoundland's Burin Peninsula. Read the following reports. The first two are parts of news reports, the third is from a report given by the relief ship, *Neigle*, of her voyage to the scene of the tidal wave disaster.

The Fisherman's Advocate
November 29, 1929

5:05 p.m. Monday, November 18, 1929
Earth tremors started, lasted 1½ minutes, buildings shaken; earth trembled.

7:35 p.m.
At first the harbours and coves went almost dry almost instantly and then the wave came in with a roaring sound. There were 2 or 3 waves but the first one came the highest.
...water fronts were stripped of all sorts of property. Boats, stores, houses and stages gone with stores of food, fuel and fishing equipment.

Newfoundland Weekly
November 23, 1929

Headline:

DISASTER IN NEWFOUNDLAND
TIDAL WAVE CAUSES DESTRUCTION TO LIFE AND PROPERTY ON SOUTH COAST

Apparently the disastrous tidal wave was an aftermath of the earthquake on Monday, that made itself felt all along the eastern Atlantic coast from New York to Newfoundland causing an ocean upheaval.

Tidal wave 15 feet (about 5 metres) high which swept away everything along the waterfront.

SOUTHWEST COAST DISASTER SUMMARY
Voyage of Relief Ship Neigle
To scene of Tidal Wave Disaster,
Lamaline to Rock Harbour,
Districts Burin East & West

Extent of coastline affected - 60 miles (about 110 kilometres)
Population affected - 10,000 people
Lives lost: 27 at the following places and to the following extent:

Port au Bras(7), Kelly's Cove(2)
Lord's Cove(4), Taylor's Bay(5),
Port au Gaul(8), Allen'Island, Lamaline(1).

Property losses, estimated at exceeding one million dollars.

Industrial effects: boats, fishing gear, supplies and other equipment of 50% of the wage earners destroyed.

Commercial effects: supplying merchants at half a dozen of the larger fishing communities stripped of property and goods rendering it impossible for them to continue in the trade.

Temperature

Of course the ocean is not at a constant temperature. It is much warmer in the tropics than in the Arctic. The temperature of the water changes as the seasons change. Inland bays are warmer than the open ocean. The temperature also changes as the water gets deeper.

Questions

12. *Does the temperature get warmer or colder as the water gets deeper?*
13. *How do ocean currents affect the ocean temperature?*

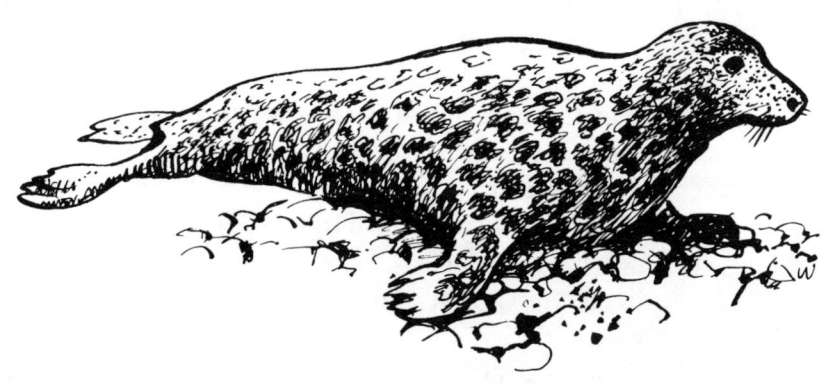

• **Something To Do**

Many artists use the ocean as a subject in their work. Look at a number of paintings of the sea or at reproductions in magazines and books. What are some different ways artists view the ocean?

ACTIVITY

Consider:
What happens when a layer of warm water is placed over a layer of cold water?

What you need:
two glass jars of the same size
red food colouring
pan (to catch the spills)
piece of cardboard, twice the size of the mouths of the jars
water

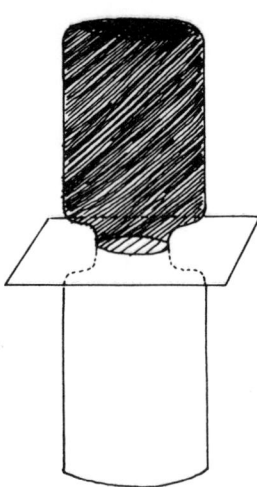

What you do:
1. Fill one jar to the top with cold water.
2. Fill the second jar to the top with warm water.
3. Add red food colouring to the warm water.
4. Wet the cardboard with water on both sides.
5. Place the cardboard over the mouth of the jar containing warm water.
6. Holding the cardboard tightly, quickly turn the jar upside down.
7. Place the jar of warm water on top of the jar of cold water.
8. Hold the jars steady and ask a friend to remove the cardboard carefully.
9. Observe what happens.

What you observed:
1. Describe what you saw. Did the warm water and cold water mix at first?
2. What happened after the jars had been sitting for 15-20 minutes? Why?

Conclusions:
1. Give reasons for what you observed happening in the experiment.
2. What do you think would happen if you *poured* the warm water over the cold? Why?
3. What do you think would happen if cold water were placed on top of warm water? Try it!

Summary

The layers of warm and cold water in this activity are similar to water layers in the ocean. Even though temperature layers exist in the ocean, there is a lot of mixing due to winds, waves, currents and tides.

Underneath the Sea

Suppose you could pump the ocean dry. What do you think you would see? You would not see a long, flat bottom. Instead you would find mountains and valleys like you see on land. Actually, the area beneath the ocean water is divided into three main regions.

The *continental shelf** is a fairly flat and shallow shelf that surrounds all the continents. A good example of a continental shelf is the Grand Banks off Newfoundland.

The shelf drops off abruptly to form the *continental slope**. Some of the slope is like a slanting mountain. Other parts plunge downward like a wall. Little sunlight can penetrate to those depths.

At the foot of the continental slope lies the ocean floor. Often called the *abyss**, this area is mysterious. In fact, humans are just beginning to explore this area. We know that it is very deep, averaging about five kilometres, and that it is made up of mountain ranges, valleys, canyons, and plateaus bigger than some of those on land. You should be able to find these on the drawing.

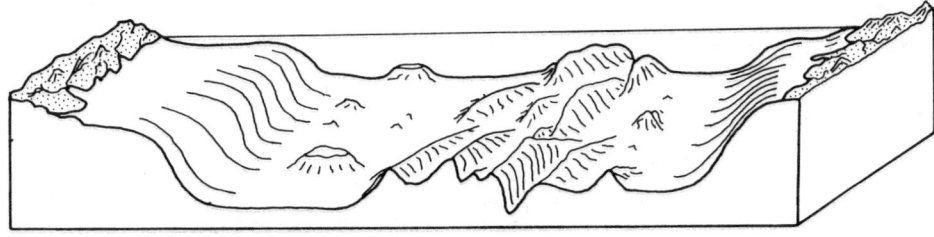

In this lesson you have studied currents, tides, waves and temperature. These are some of the physical or non-living conditions of the ocean.

Questions

14. *Where do you think the warmer water would be in the ocean?*
15. *Do you think the physical conditions of the continental shelf are the same as those of the abyss? Give reasons for your answer.*

You have learned about the physical conditions of the ocean. These conditions affect the environment in which plants and animals live. Temperature for instance, affects what food is available and where an animal will travel. Can we grow pineapples in Newfoundland? Could a tropical fish like a barracuda survive off Labrador? The wind affects birds' flight, ocean waves, weather patterns and places plants can grow. The non-living parts of the ocean constantly affect all the living parts, the plants and animals. Think of a few more ways the physical conditions influence the ocean's organisms.

In the next lesson, we'll learn more about what living things need to survive, and why they live in certain environments.

Special Activity

> # OCEANOGRAPHER
>
> See how many words you can make using any combination of letters found in the word oceanographer. (One champ found 21 different words!)

NEW WORDS

abyss
    the ocean floor at the base of the continental slope

continental shelf
    the relatively shallow portion of seabed bordering most continents, usually no more than 100 fathoms (188 metres) deep

continental slope
    the slope beyond a continental shelf which descends steeply to deeper water

current
    water that is moving along in a path

gravitational force
    attraction between one mass and another

neap tide
    the lowest tide, when the moon is in its first or last quarter

ocean wave
    a curving or rippling movement on the surface of the ocean

oceanographer
    a scientist who studies the physical properties of the ocean

seismic wave
    wave caused by an earthquake or other movement of the earth's crust, an usually high destructive wave, called tidal wave in the United States, *Tsunami* in Japan

spring tide
    the highest tide, when the moon is full or new

Lesson 2

LIFE IN THE OCEAN

What do ocean plants and animals need?

The ocean world is made up of living and non-living things. We have learned about some of the non-living things. What about the living things? What do they need to survive? Where in the ocean do they live? Why?

Nutrients* and *sunlight* are two of the most important factors that influence the survival of any living thing.

Nutrients

All living things, plants, animals and even you, need nutrients to survive. Nutrients help living things grow and develop. Vitamins and minerals are examples of nutrients.

Animals get nutrients from the food they eat. When we eat a balance of meat and vegetables, we get the necessary nutrients to stay healthy. Plants do it differently. Plants make their own food by capturing some of the sun's energy and using ingredients from the soil, water and air. Plants and their nutrients are then eaten by animals.

Here are some sources of nutrients in the ocean.

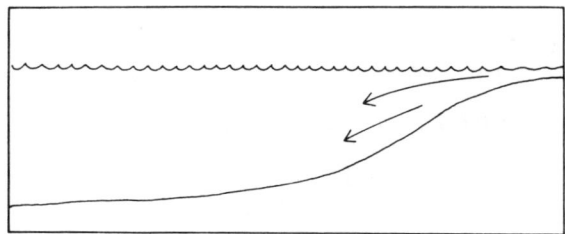

1. Some minerals are found on the ocean bottom in sedimentary deposits*. The minerals come from soil and rocks carried to the ocean by rivers.

2. Some nutrients found in the ocean come from animal waste.

3. Decaying* organisms are another important source of nutrients in the ocean.

Does this garbage decay and provide nutrients?

11

ACTIVITY

Consider:

What properties of nutrients and the ocean cause an uneven distribution of nutrients? How does this affect the organisms which live on them?

What you need:

cooking oil
water
glass jar with lid
rice, barley, or similar sized grain
bran

What to do:

1. Pour cold water into the jar until it is two-thirds full.
2. Add enough oil to cover the surface of the water completely. (The oil and water represent two layers of water in the ocean.)
3. Throw on the bran.
4. Put in barley. Allow it to settle. (The bran and barley represent two different kinds of nutrients.)
5. Shake and let settle again.

What you observed:

1. Did the layers of liquid mix?
2. After they settled, where were the nutrients?
3. What happened to the liquids and the nutrients after you shook the jar?

Conclusions:

1. If some marine organisms were feeding mainly on bran, in what layer would you find them?
2. If they were feeding continuously on bran, what would happen to the amount of bran? What problems would this cause?

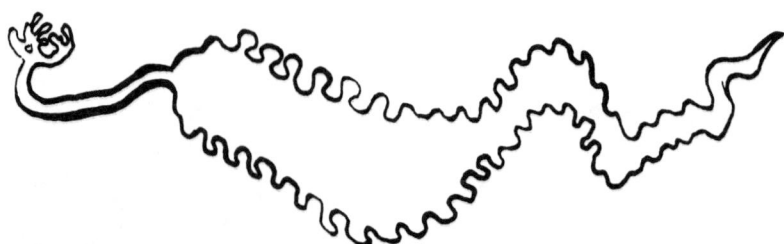

Summary

Because of various factors, such as currents, waves and temperature, nutrients are not distributed evenly throughout the ocean. This means that organisms must live where the nutrients they need are found.

Distribution of nutrients

Nutrients are distributed in the ocean in a variety of ways. In some places, the wind pushes the surface water out to sea and deeper water moves up to take its place. This is called *upwelling**. Upwelling brings a lot of nutrients to the top layer of the ocean. Lots of plants and animals live where upwelling takes place. If it were not for upwelling currents and waves, the nutrients in the top layer of the ocean would soon run out. Without nutrients, the organisms would die. The ocean layers must mix so that nutrients rise.

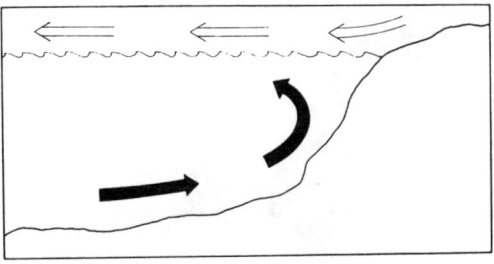

Question

1. *How can currents and waves help mix up the ocean layers?*

Sunlight

The sun is the most important factor for life on our planet. All living things depend in some way on the sun's energy.

Plants in the ocean need sunlight to survive, just as plants on land do. The problem is, the rays of the sun can only reach down so far. If you visited the ocean depths, you would notice that very little light reaches the ocean floor. In fact, you'd probably want to take an underwater flashlight with you to find your way about. It is so dark on much of the ocean floor that some animals make their own light. The lanternfish, for example, lives in the deep sea and has organs that produce light to help it see in the deep, dark waters. Do you think many plants live in the deep sea? In the great depths of the ocean there are no plants at all. Generally, most of the ocean plant life lives in the upper layers of water, that is, no deeper than 100 metres. Here they can capture the sunlight they need.

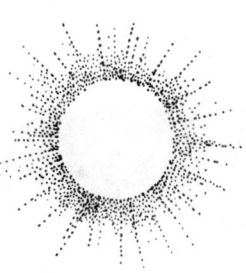

Question

2. *Look at the diagram of the ocean profile (page 9, Lesson 1). Where do you think most animals would live? Why?*

Plants and Animals of the Ocean

There is a great variety of living things in the ocean, more than we can study in this book. The most common organisms are *plankton*. Plankton are small plants and animals most of which you can't see without a microscope.

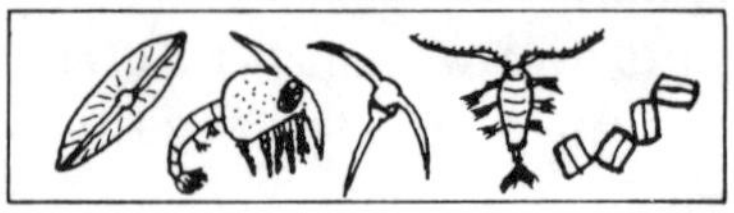

• Something to do

These are some of the organisms that live in the ocean. Some swim in the water; some live on the ocean floor; some just come to feed. Can you identify them? When you have finished, check your answers with the list at the end of this chapter.

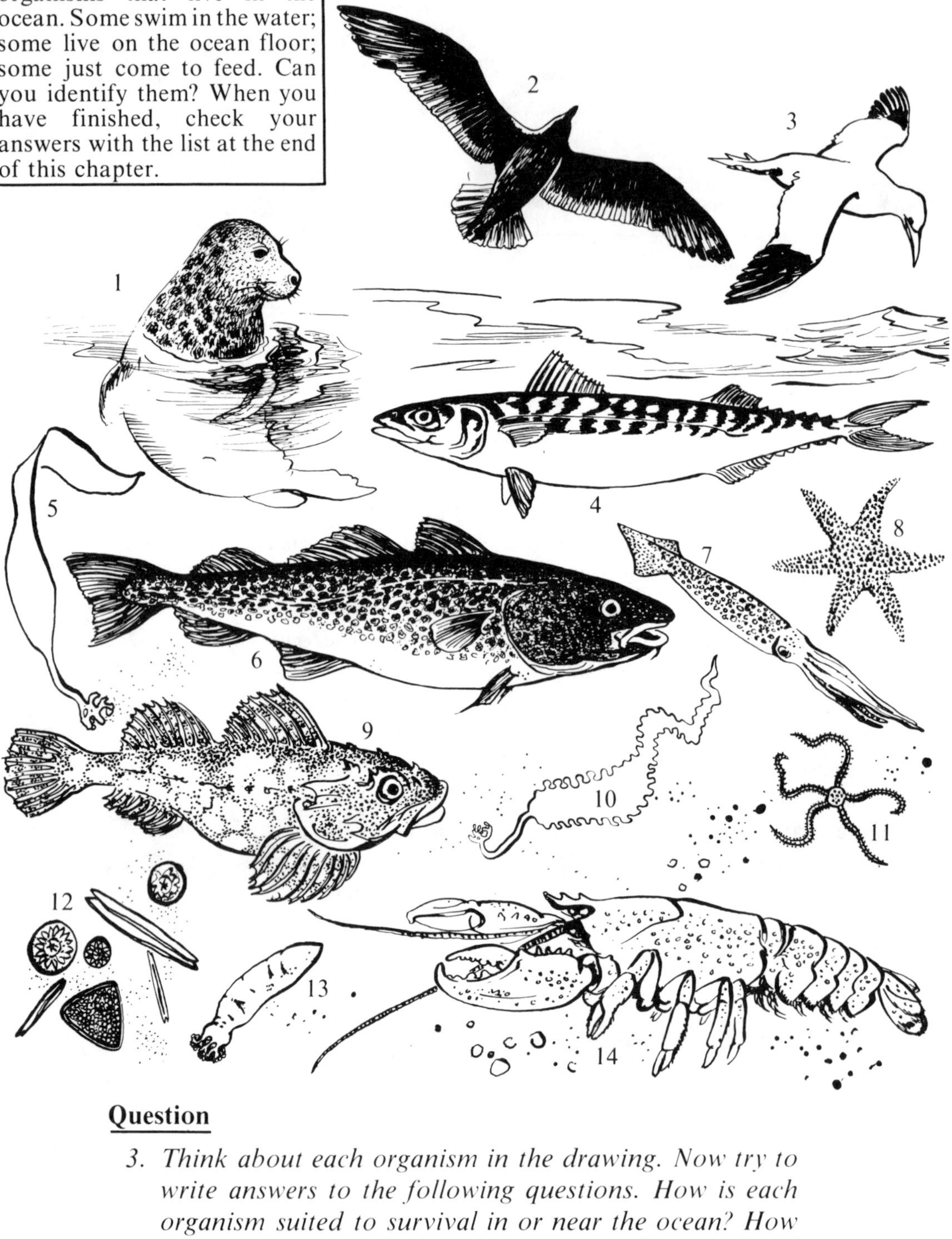

Question

3. Think about each organism in the drawing. Now try to write answers to the following questions. How is each organism suited to survival in or near the ocean? How does it move? How does it get nutrients? Who eats whom?

You can see that there are lots of places in the ocean to live. In the next lesson, you will learn about where certain organisms live and why they live where they do.

SPECIAL ACTIVITY

The ocean words listed below are hidden in this puzzle. Find them and circle them. Words may be written left to right, right to left, diagonally or up and down.

```
s o s a o c b f c u r r e n t
e n e s s y p n o t k n a l p
a e d d e i f i t a r t s h i
l t u n a r f c s u j h q k s
w t p k w h o w b p f g u m y
b m i c e d o s o w q i i b r
n b o d e v d o l e r l d o a
w t o v d x l a t l p n c c t
i d a s w a h m t l c e e h n
n w j s q u i d h i a s p t e
d r r l s t r w g n e e u k m
w l f e d c a h i g h g o n i
b e d o t k n a l p f s l n d
c i c n i v o l e y g r e n e
t r n u t r i e n t s j b l s
```

OCEAN WORDS

squid	whale	cod
nutrients	upwelling	seaweed
tuna	wind	sedimentary
sun	food	current
seal	light	ocean
wave	tides	energy
plankton		squid

15

NEW WORDS

decaying
    slow rotting

nutrients
    food, substances needed by people, animals and plants for life and growth.

sedimentary deposits
    rock particles and other materials that have settled in layers at the bottom of water.

upwelling
    the rising of nutrient-rich waters from the ocean depths to the surface, often caused by wind.

Living Things shown on page 14:

1. Seal   2. Seagull   3. Gannet   4. Mackerel
5. Seaweed   6. Cod   7. Squid   8. Starfish
9. Sculpin   10. Seaweed   11. Brittle Star   12. Plankton
13. Sea Cucumber   14. Lobster

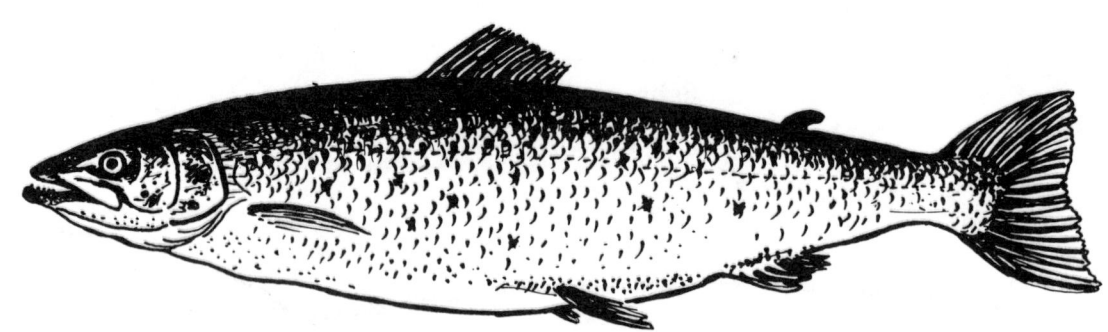

Lesson 3

THE WEB OF LIFE

What would it be like to live in the ocean?

Imagine yourself living in a world of water. Everything around you is constantly moving. There is not much light and the water is salty. These are some of the physical characteristics of your watery home. Who else lives there? There are many different plants and animals, small and large. Together, these living and non-living things form the ocean environment.

Habitat

An animal's habitat is the place in which it lives and grows. It is the particular part of the environment which fulfills the needs of the animal, providing its food, shelter and protection. An animal's habitat is its neighbourhood or *address*.

Do you have a habitat? Think about your shelter, where you get your food and water, and where you carry out your daily activities. This is the area that makes up your habitat.

Question

1. What does every organism need to survive? It's habitat must supply these needs. Describe your own habitat and how all your needs are met.

17

The size of an organism's habitat depends on its needs. Habitats of different organisms often overlap. A field mouse's habitat includes the field in which it lives, its nest and the grasses and grains it eats. A cow might live in the same field but its habitat is much larger than the habitat of the field mouse. The cow's habitat includes the neighbouring fields and woods and a barn stall. What other organisms might share the habitats of the mouse and the cow?

This diagram illustrates habitats of different sizes and shows how they overlap.

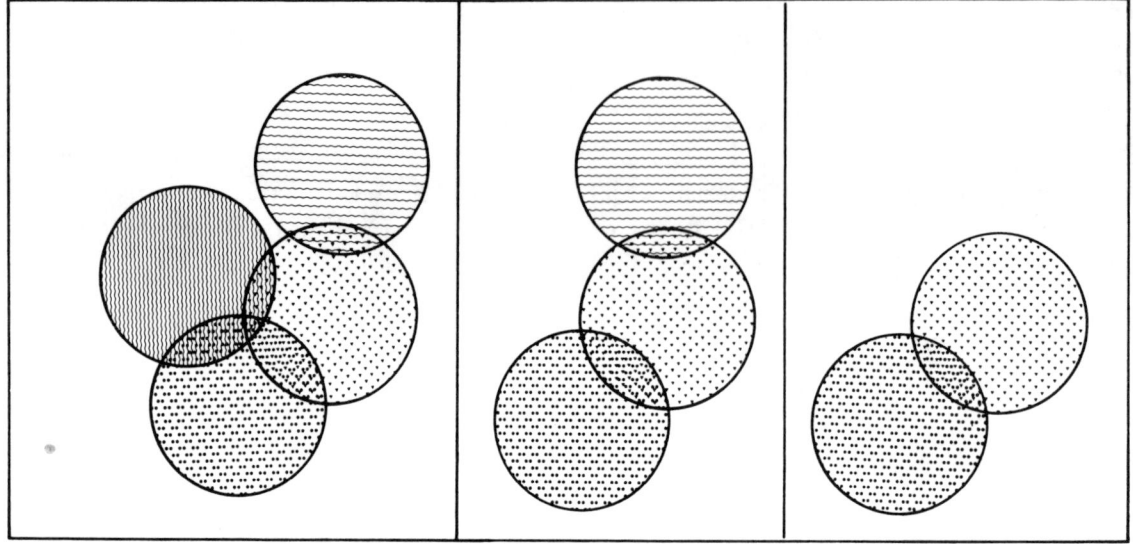

Question

2. Do you share your habitat with other organisms? List all those you can think of.

Ocean Habitats

The ocean environment provides habitats for many different organisms. Look again at the picture of organisms in the ocean in Lesson 2 on page 14. Some of these organisms, such as the sculpin and the seaweeds, live near the shore. The brittle star and the sea cucumber live on the ocean floor. Other organisms, like the squid and the mackerel, live in the open water. Where do the other organisms shown in the drawing live?

A mussel has a very small habitat. It stays in the same place for its whole life. Mussels eat plankton, which they filter out of the water around them.

18

The whale has a very large habitat. Whales need to travel far to find all they need to live. When an animal travels a long distance for a purpose, this is called migrating.

Humpback whales migrate long distances. Each year, they swim from cold, Arctic waters to warm, tropical waters. Humpbacks can be see around Newfoundland and Labrador in the summer feeding on capelin and krill. There is lots of food in our cold, nutrient-rich waters, so it's worthwhile for the whales to travel all this way. Humpbacks need warm water in which to bear their young. So in winter they stop feeding and migrate to the Caribbean, where the baby humpbacks (or calves) are born. Humpback whales only feed for about half of each year. How would you like to eat for only half of each year.

As you can see, the habitat of the humpback whale is very large because the conditions it needs for survival are far apart.

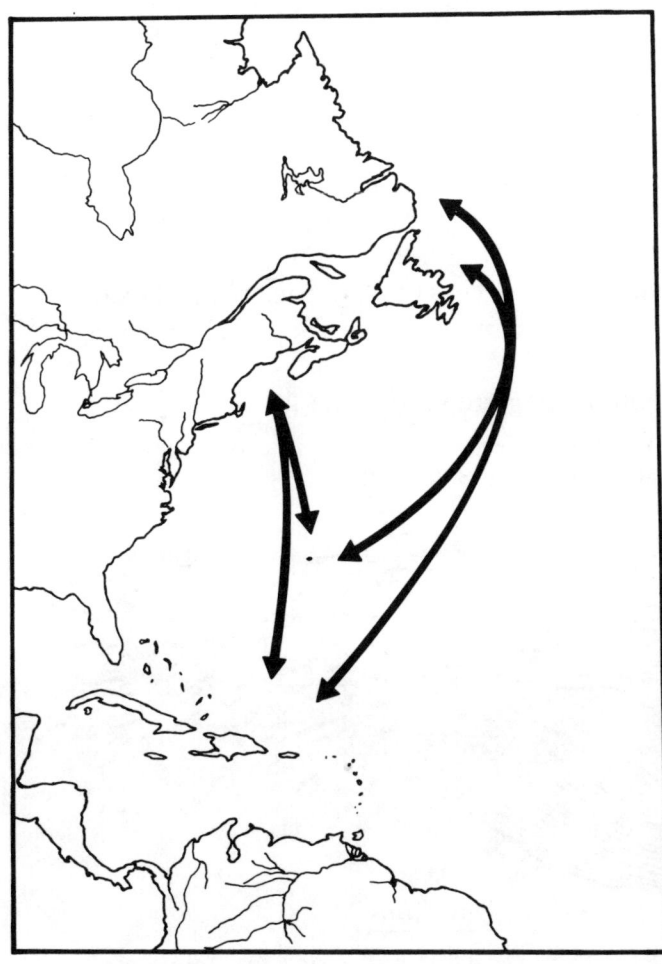

Question

3. How big is the habitat of a humpback from one end of its migration to the other? Use the scale to find out the distance (in kilometres).

Niche

Each type of organism in a habitat has a special role to play. An organism's role in the environment is called its *niche*. The niche of an organism depends on where it lives and particularly on what it does. The niche is like the organism's *job*. For example, the role or niche of a cod, the *predator**, is to eat capelin, the *prey**, and to be eaten by man and other animals. Cod is a *consumer**, an organism which eats other living things.

Look at the example below. The arrows go from the prey to the predator each time.

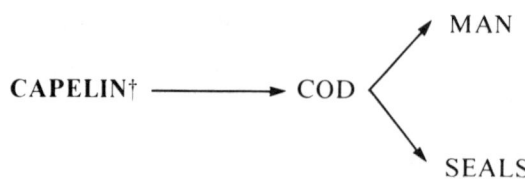

The capelin is the prey when the cod is the predator.

The cod is the prey when seals and man are predators.

We know that every organism lives in a certain place and eats certain foods. Some animals live on or in another organism. Some barnacles live on whales and travel wherever the whale goes. They filter their food out of the water in the same way barnacles that are attached to rocks do. Some types of worms live inside whales and seals. Other organisms eat animals or the waste products of animals. The many different types of animal plankton filter through the waste products of whales and fish to take out the nutrients they need.

Plants have niches too. Kelp is a *producer**, some types of plankton are producers too. A producer uses sunlight, water and nutrients to make its own food. Kelp is eaten by a consumer such as a sea urchin.

The niche of a ten year old student might be to go to school and learn, and to eat the proper food to grow and stay healthy.

What would be the niche of a large animal such as a whale?

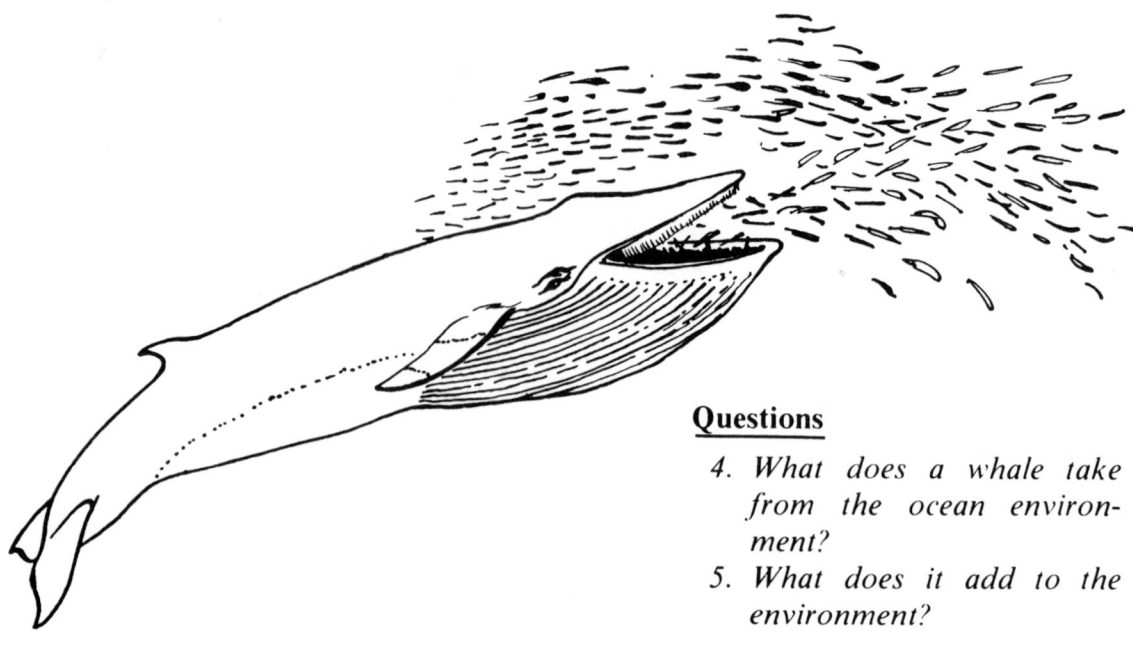

Questions

4. What does a whale take from the ocean environment?
5. What does it add to the environment?

†In Newfoundland, *capelin*, is also spelled *caplin*.

As we have said, the niche of an organism is its role in the environment. Its role is defined by what it eats and what eats it! The food of all organisms comes from plants. Animals may eat plants directly or they may eat them indirectly, by eating other animals that eat plants.

Food Chains

Question

6. Make a list of the things you ate for supper yesterday. Identify which ones come from plants and which ones come from animals. For the ones which come from animals, make a list of things that the animal eats. If it eats other animals, list the things those animals eat. Now trace a path to the sun. Continue until each list of foods ends with the sun.

Example:

MACARONI AND CHEESE

MACARONI ⟶ WHEAT (flour)

CHEESE ⟶ COW ⟶ GRAIN

You have now created a list of *food chains**! A food chain shows how plants and animals are related in their niches. One living thing depends on another for food. Here is an example of a food chain.

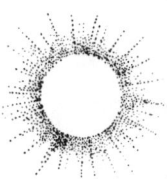

SUN ⟶ PLANKTON ⟶ KRILL ⟶ CAPELIN ⟶ COD ⟶ HUMANS

Question

7. Describe another food chain from the ocean, by arranging these organisms in their proper order: mussel, sun, starfish, plankton, cunner (or conner - a small fish).

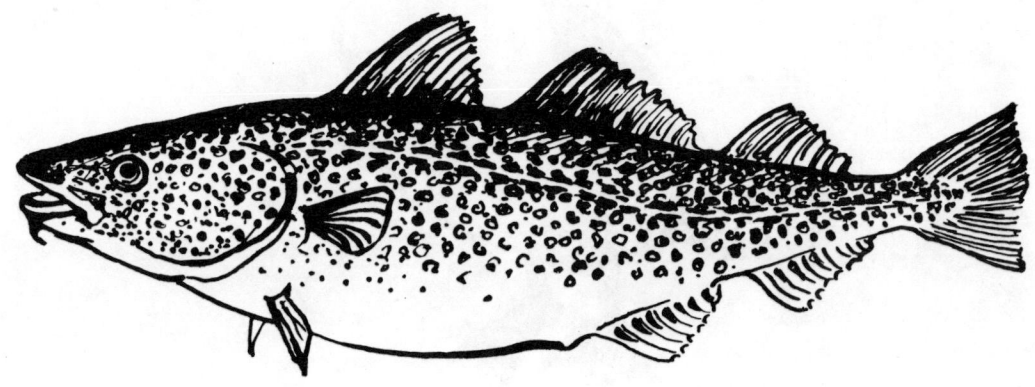

Food Webs

Are you a link in a food chain? Are you part of many food chains? Most food chains have one or more links in common with other food chains. This makes what is called a *food web**. Food webs are very complicated, because everything is related or interdependent, either directly or indirectly.

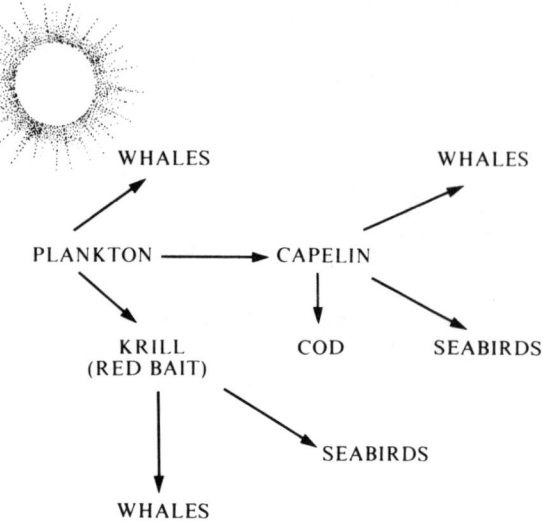

Some whales eat small fish, such as capelin and krill. What do the small fish eat?

Some whales eat tiny plankton which they filter out of the water. All whales depend on plants for their food. Plants depend on the sun.

Cod and seabirds are also members of this ocean food web. Are human beings members too? Where do we belong?

Questions

8. What is a producer in the food web pictured above?
9. Find and list as many three-link food chains from the above web as you can. For example: plankton ⟶ capelin ⟶ seabirds. Which ones could include humans?

ACTIVITY:
(Food Web Game)

Consider:

How are living and non-living parts of the environment interdependent?

What you need:

ball of yarn
name tags
ten or more people

What to do:

1. As a class, make a *recipe* for an ocean. What are the ingredients that must go into an ocean? Remember to include both living and non-living things.
2. Put the recipe on the blackboard. Choose something from the recipe you would like to be. Write your name next to it and make a nametag for yourself. Put it on.
3. Everyone in the class should sit in a circle.
4. One person takes the ball of yarn, holds the end and passes the ball to someone he or she influences. For example, *cod* might pass the ball to *capelin*. *Capelin* would take hold of the yarn and pass the ball to *plankton*. *Plankton* might pass it to *sun*. Continue until everyone is connected to at least one other person. (One person can be connected to many others.) The yarn should be tangled up like a web.

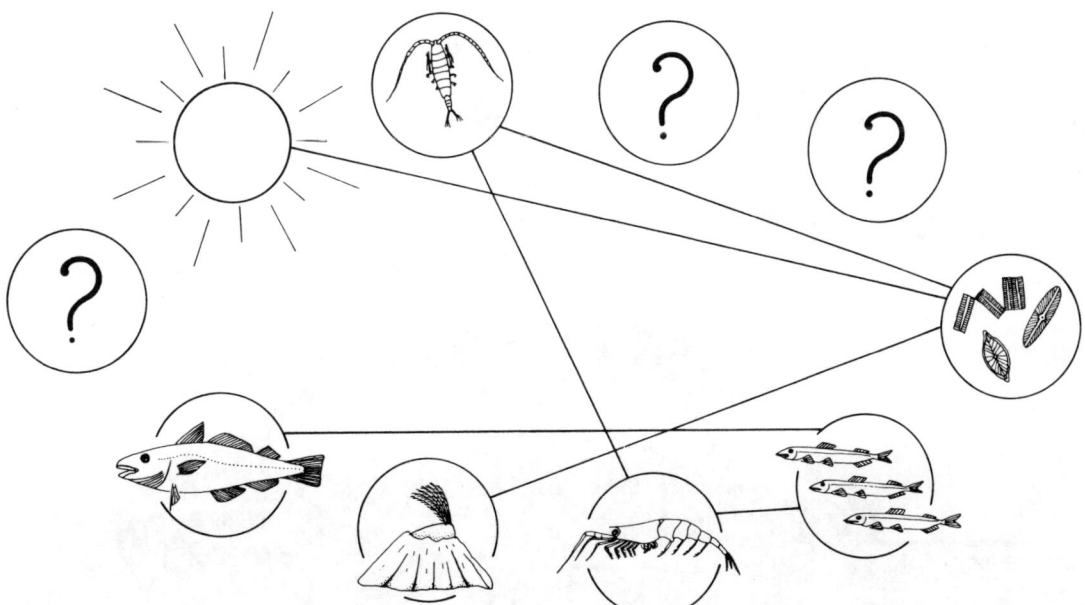

5. Have one person in your food web stand up and, holding the piece of yarn, back away from the circle.

What you observed:

1. What happened when one thing was removed from the food web? What else was affected? Why?

Conclusion:

1. Write two food chains of four links each from the web your class made.

Summary

By using the yarn to connect parts of an ocean food web, you have seen how one part depends on others for survival. You might imagine what happens to the parts of the food web when one part is eliminated.

We have learned about the living and non-living parts of the ocean. The ocean is very complex because its parts are constantly interacting. In order to understand the ocean better, we will look at whales as an example of an organism which lives in the ocean.

NEW WORDS

consumer
    an organism that has to feed on other living things, example: fish, whales and fishermen

food chain
    a series of links that shows one organism eating another

food web
    a complicated network of food chains

predator
    an organism which feeds by capturing and killing other organisms

prey
    an organism hunted or killed for food by another organism

producer
    an organism that makes its own food, example: most plants

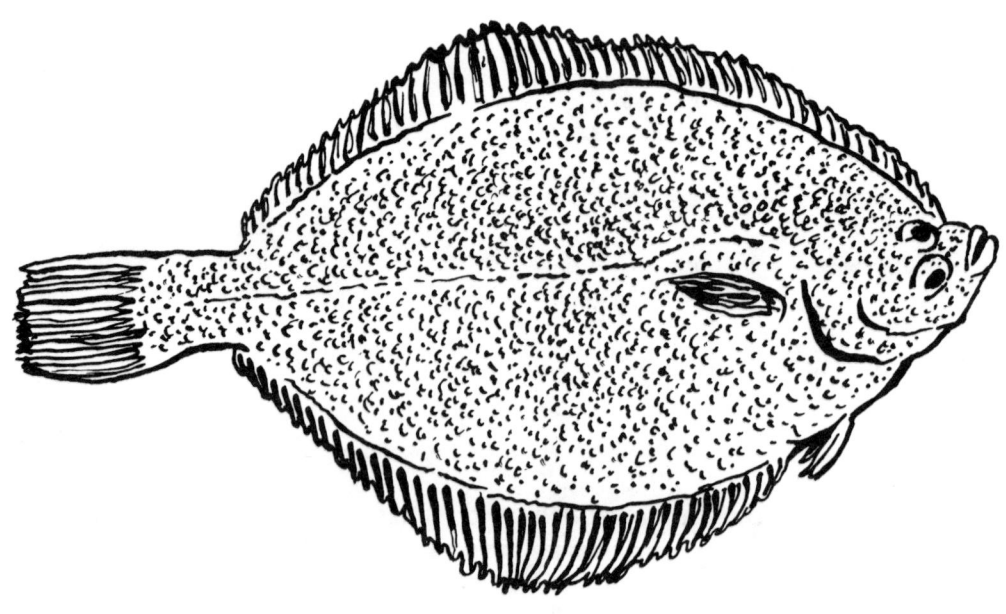

Lesson 4

WHAT IS A WHALE?

Did you know that whales are not fish?

Whales are one of the kinds of organisms that live in the sea. They are often seen in the waters off Newfoundland and Labrador during the summer months. Whales are mammals as we are, yet they spend their lives in the water.

Do you remember the characteristics of mammals? You might want to review them in your science textbook.

Questions

1. Make a list of the characteristics of mammals.
2. Make a chart using the headings given below. Fill in as many points as you can think of under each heading.

HUMANS AND WHALES

Differences　　　　　　　　　　**Similarities**

Are all these living things mammals?

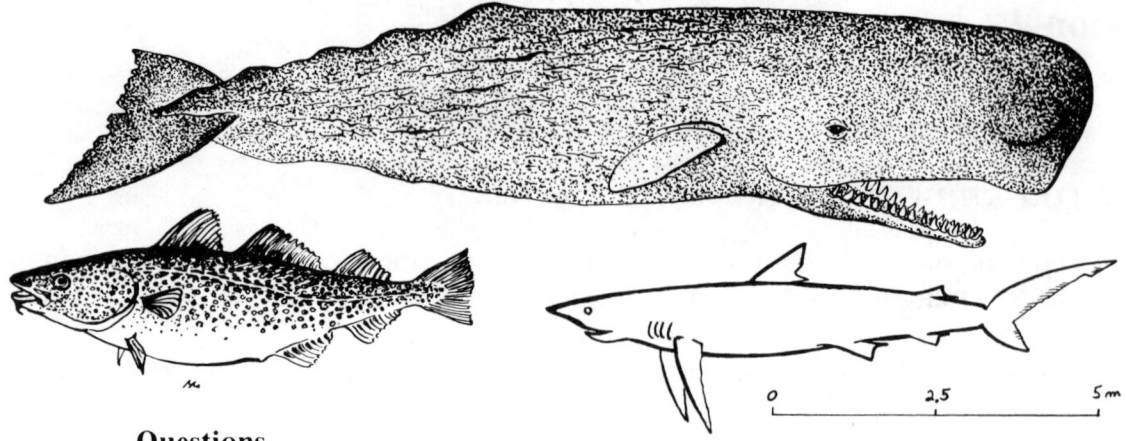

Questions

3. Look at the tails of the fish and the whale. How are they different?
4. What other differences can you see between the whale and fish?
5. Is the shark more like a fish or a whale? How?

Adaptations

Each organism has special characteristics which help it survive in its environment. These characteristics are called *adaptations**. For example, birds have wings and feathers which help them fly. Fish have gills for breathing in water. Bears have fur which keeps them warm. These are all adaptations. Each organism shows special adaptation to its habitat and niche. Whales are mammals adapted to their ocean habitat and niche.

> **• Something to do**
>
> Get a partner. Have your partner tape your thumbs to the rest of your hands. Then have your partner time you while he or she tries to do some of these things:
>
> — open and close a zipper on a pencil case or jacket
> — fasten a buckle or safety pin
> — write two words
> — open a door
> — turn five pages of a book
> — button a sweater or coat
>
> Now have your "untaped" partner try the same things while *you* time. How much faster can he or she do them?

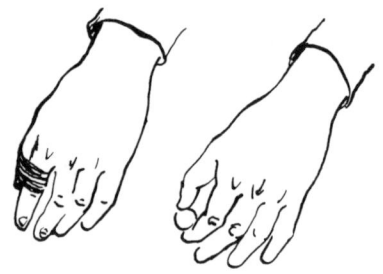

Humans are adapted to their environment too. Most animals do not have hands like ours. One of our adaptations is the thumb. You just have seen how important the thumb is in our everyday lives. How would you like to live without it?

Think of the problems humans might have living in the sea. The ocean is cold; how would we keep warm? How would we breathe? What would happen if we tried to eat underwater? How would we find our friends and talk to them under water? How would we move around easily?

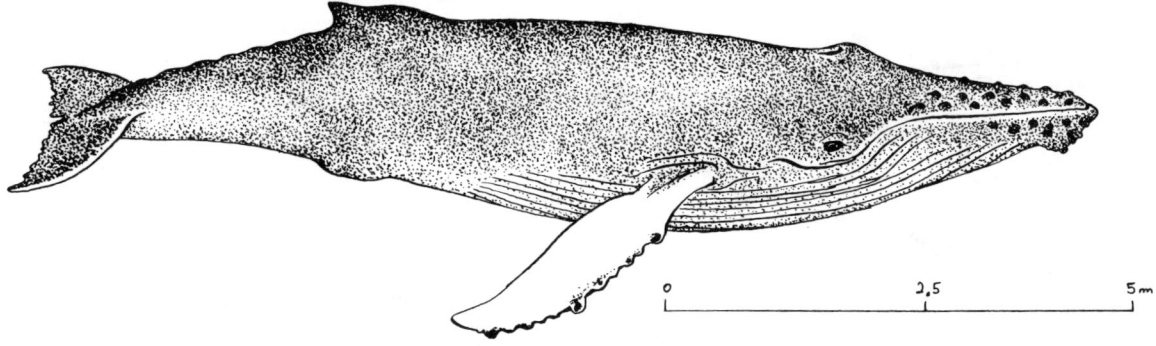

Adaptations of the Whale

In the rest of this lesson, we will be taking a closer look at the whale to see how it is adapted to live in its environment. We will consider the importance of its large size, how it keeps warm, feeds, breathes and reproduces. This diagram can be used as a guide.

Size

Most whales are large. The blue whale is extra-large. It is the biggest animal that has ever lived on earth. A blue whale can grow as long as 30 metres and have a masse of 135 tonnes. Blue whales are much larger than elephants or even the largest dinosaur, the brontosaurus.

ACTIVITY

Consider:

How long is a whale?

What you need:

metre stick
pencil   paper

What you do:

1. Measure yourself using the metre stick.
2. Look at the diagram of the humpback whale above. A scale is given. Use the scale to find out how long the humpback whale is.

What you observed:

1. How long are you?
2. How long is the whale?
3. How many people, the same length as you, lined up lying head to toe, would it take to equal the length of the humpback whale?
4. Now try these same measurements using the *blue whale* diagram on page 28.

Conclusion:

1. Write a paragraph telling how you would feel if you were as big as a whale? How would you feel if you couldn't see your feet? What problems would your size cause you? You might want to include a scaled drawing of you (big as a whale) next to your house and family.

Summary

Through this activity you have gained a clearer understanding of the vast size of the whale and its ocean environment.

You now have a clear idea of how big whales are compared to you and your world. But the important question is *why* are whales so large? How is a whale's large size useful to it? For one thing, the bigger you are, the more food energy you can store in your body. As you know, some whales only feed for half of the year. Storing food energy is important. Also, when you are as big as a whale, fewer animals are likely to hunt you for food. One of the most important benefits of the whale's large size is in keeping the animal warm in cold ocean waters. This is important for the whale because unlike most sea creatures, it is warm-blooded and must maintain a constant temperature. The next activity will help you understand how size and keeping warm are connected.

ACTIVITY

Consider:
Which cools off faster, large things or small things?

What you need:
two containers of different sizes
hot water
thermometer

What you do:
1. Fill each container with hot water.
2. Record the temperature of the water in each container every five minutes for fifteen minutes.
3. Make a table like this one and fill it in.

Time	Temperature of water in large container	Temperature of water in small container
at begining	⁰C	⁰C
at five minutes	⁰C	⁰C
at ten minutes	⁰C	⁰C
at fifteen minutes	⁰C	⁰C

What you observed:
1. Which container became cool faster?

Conclusions:
1. Why do you think the water in one container cooled faster than the water in the other container?
2. Would it be easier for a large whale or a small whale to keep warm?

Summary

Large bodies lose heat more slowly than small bodies. The large size of most whales helps keep them warm. Small whales must be active to stay warm.

Whale Movement

In the ocean whales can float. The water supports their huge bodies, just as it supports humans when we swim. This means that even though whales grow very large, they can move easily. They don't have to carry their weight on legs as we do. Our bodies are suited for walking. Whales' bodies are suited for swimming.

Whales have many adaptations to swimming in the ocean. They are *streamlined** so that they can move easily through the water. They do not have shoulders which would slow them down. Also, whales have smooth skin and very little hair. This means there is little *resistance** to the flow of water around the whale as it moves.

Questions

6. How could human bodies be better suited for swimming? What parts would you change?

7. Why do you think some swimmers shave their heads when they race in important competitions like the Olympics?

A whale's tail, called *flukes**, is used for swimming. The flukes are very powerful. A killer whale can swim as fast as 50 kilometres per hour!

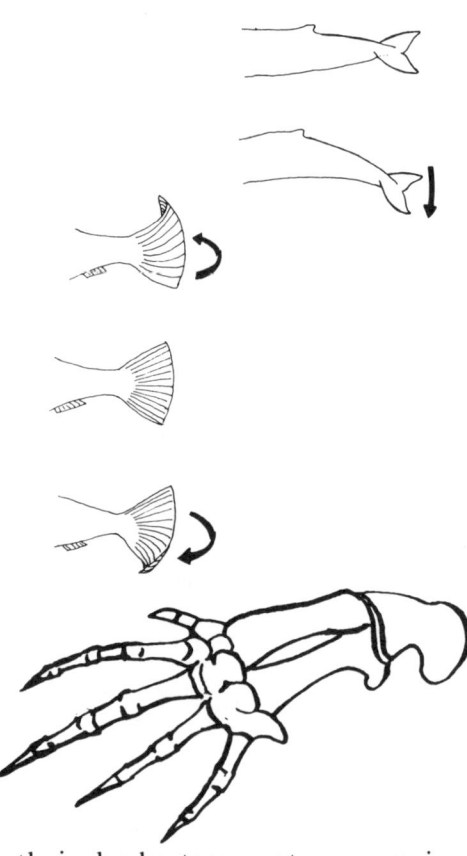

- **Something to do:**

Tape a small piece of paper to a pencil. Pretend the pencil is the backbone and the paper is the tail of a fish or whale. First move it like a fish's tail moves when swimming and then like a whale's tail. Whales and fish, as you have discovered, have very different swimming methods.

The *flippers** help the whale keep its balance. They also help the whale turn or change direction. What part of the human body do the flippers look like?

Keeping Warm

All mammals are warm-blooded. This means their body temperature remains constant. Whales can live in cold arctic waters and in warm tropical waters. Their body temperature does not change even when the water temperature changes. Besides their size, whales have another important adaptation which helps them keep warm. This is a thick layer of fat, called *blubber**. It is located just below the skin. Unlike most land mammals, whales do not have a thick fur coat. Blubber also stores food and helps to maintain *buoyancy**, to keep the animal floating.

ACTIVITY

Consider:
What would happen to whales if they did not have blubber?

What you need:
a pot of very cold water
four plastic bags
¼ kilogram lard

What you do:
1. Put the lard into a plastic bag spreading it so it coats the inside of the bag.
2. Put the bag of lard into the pot of cold water, keeping the mouth of the bag above water so the bag does not fill with water.
3. Put each of your hands into one of the other plastic bags.
4. Put one hand into the bag of lard.
5. Put the other hand into another bag and put it into the water.

What you observed:
1. Did one hand feel colder than the other? Which one?
2. What do you think would happen to your hands if you left them in longer?

Conclusions:
1. What difference did the lard make? Did it insulate your hand?
2. What do whales have to protect them from cold water?
3. Why do you think you put one hand into the water without lard?

Summary
The lard in this experiment acts like a layer of blubber to keep one hand warm.

Question
8. *List three characteristics of whales which help them keep warm.*

Breathing

Mammals living on land, as we do, seldom have any trouble breathing. But think of how much more difficult it is for you to breath when you're swimming. Whales live all their lives in the water. They must regularly come to the surface to get air. Their bodies are well designed for this, as their nostrils are located on the tops of their heads. A whale has one or two nostrils which are also called *blowholes*. Around each blowhole is a set of powerful lip muscles, which can close off the hole to prevent water from entering when the whale dives.

"Thar she blows, Skipper!" is a salty saying used by sailors when they sight a whale blowing. Whenever a whale surfaces it must exhale the old air and breathe in a lungful of fresh air. A whale's spout, or blow, is simply its breath being exhaled. As the warm air is being exhaled from the whales's lungs, it meets the cooler, outside air and condenses. This forms a fine spray. Have you ever seen your breath on a cold day? This is the same process: warm air from inside your lungs meets cold air on the outside. Part of the blow may also be water that was trapped in the nostril when the whale dove. As the whale surfaces and exhales, this trapped water is forced out under great pressure and forms spray.

Not only can you see a whale blow, you can hear it too! On calm days especially, the sound of a blow will carry for many kilometres. When a whale blows, the air being forced in and out quickly makes a loud wooshing sound. In the summertime around Newfoundland and Labrador you can often see the blows of whales from shore.

● **Something to do**

1. Place your hands on top of your head to form a large blowhole.
2. Next take a deep breath in through your mouth, close your hands tightly, squat and imagine you are underwater.
3. After 15-20 seconds, stand up, open your hands and quickly exhale and then inhale strongly, close your hands tightly, submerge and repeat.

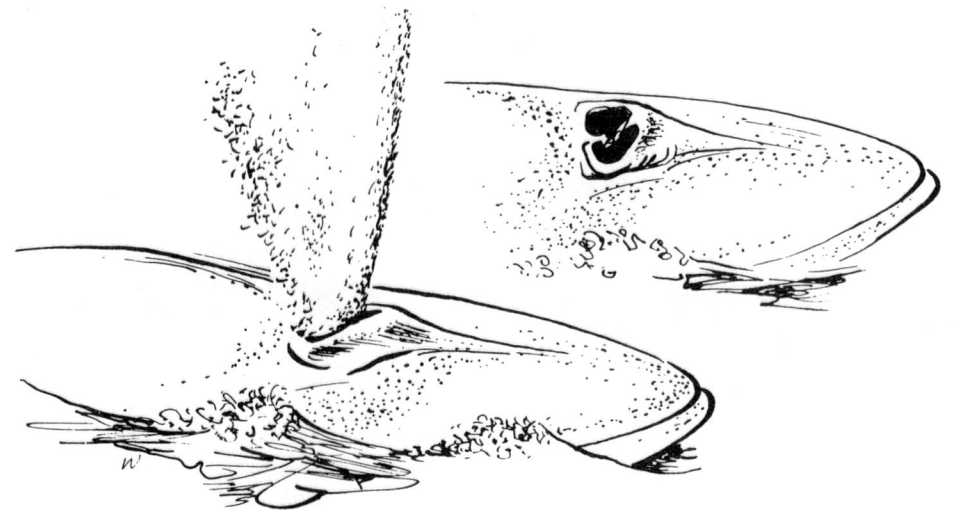

Feeding

All animals have to eat. Animals in the ocean have many different ways of feeding themselves.

Different kinds of whales feed in different ways. Some whales have teeth and some do not. The toothed whales do not chew their food, they swallow it in chunks. This is because their teeth are well adapted for biting but not for grinding or chewing. The teeth of different whales are different sizes depending on the size of the food the whale most commonly eats. Many toothed whales feed on squid or fish. Killer whales also eat seals and other kinds of whales.

Question

9. *How are our teeth different from those of a toothed whale?*

The common *toothed whales* in Newfoundland and Labrador include: the killer whale, sperm whale, pothead whale, white-beaked dolphin (or squidhound), the white-sided dolphin (or jumper) and the harbour porpoise (or puffing pig).

People studying whales have found that they can determine the age of a whale by counting the rings of a tooth. Each ring represents one year of growth. This is the same method that is used to age many living things. How can we tell how old a tree is?

This diagram is a cross-section of a tooth from a whale. The tooth was cut through the middle from tip to base.

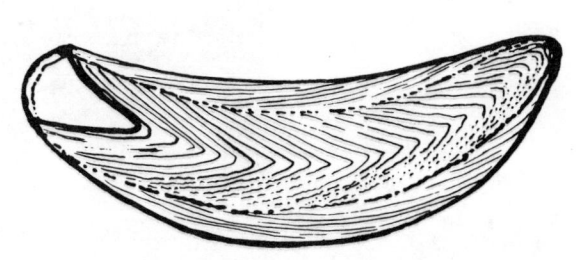

Some whales do not have teeth at all! They have a material called *baleen** which helps them feed. It hangs in hair-like plates from the roof of the mouth. It acts like a strainer when the whale is eating. The whale takes in large gulps of water. Mixed in with the water are many small fish, such as capelin, or shrimp-like plankton called krill. The whale has special pleats or grooves in its throat, so it can make it bigger. They are called *ventral grooves* because they are found on the underside or ventral side of the whale. As the whale is feeding, these grooves enlarge, so the whale can take in a huge amount of food and water in one gulp. It then closes its mouth. The tongue forces the water out of the mouth but the baleen holds the food in. The food is then swallowed. Although the mouth may be very large, the throat is no larger than a grapefruit. In one meal, a blue whale eats enough krill to provide a person with breakfast, dinner, and supper for three years!

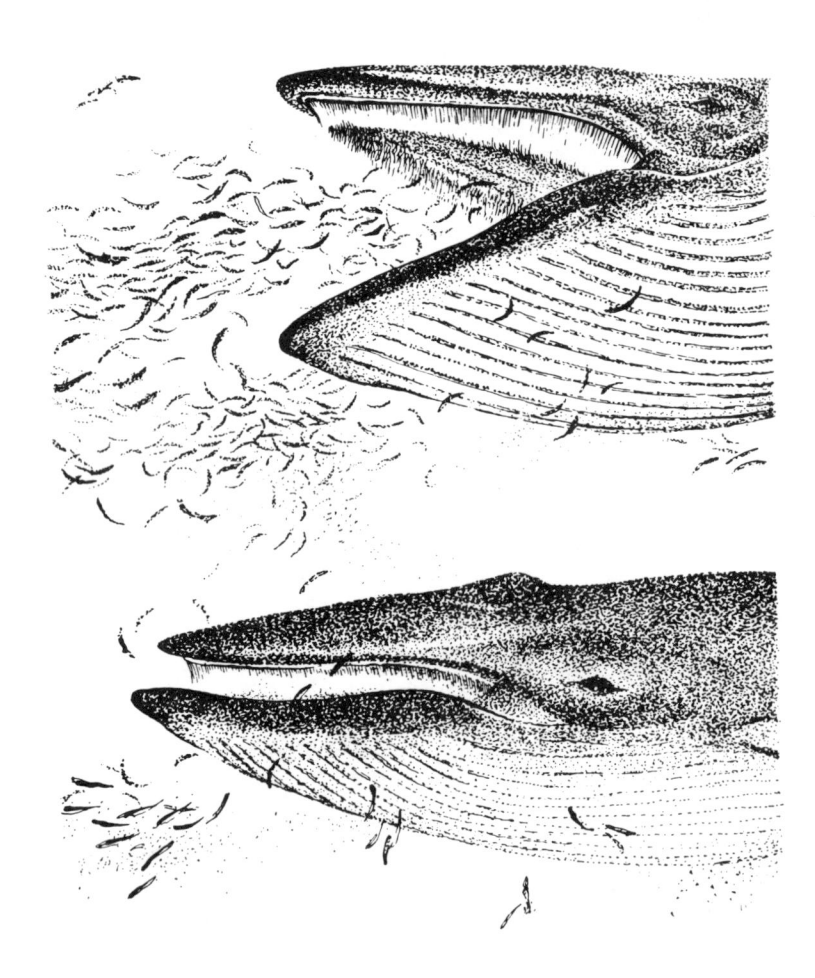

The common baleen whales seen around Newfoundland and Labrador include: the **humpback whale**, the **minke whale** (grampus), and the **finback whale** (fin, finner).

Whale Sounds

Animals often live in groups. When they do, they need to *communicate* or exchange information with one another. This type of communicating is called *social communication*. Some animals, such as bats and toothed whales, use sound to locate objects. This is called *echolocation.**

Communication may involve only one sense, such as hearing, sight or touch, or it may depend on a variety of senses.

Question

10. *If you lived in the ocean, what problems would you have in communicating with other people? How would you do it?*

Some communication methods work better in one habitat than in another. Whales depend mainly on their sense of hearing to communicate. This is probably because it is difficult to see in the darkness of the ocean. Sounds travel easily through water.

A variety of sounds is produced by whales. Some are very high-pitched sounds which humans can't hear. These are used for navigation, finding their way around, and for the location of food and other objects. To locate an object, the whale produces a series of clicking sounds. If the sounds reach an object, an echo is produced which tells the whale the location, size, movement and physical qualities of the object. By putting together the echoes, the whale forms a "picture" of the object. This ability is called *echolocation* and is used by toothed whales.

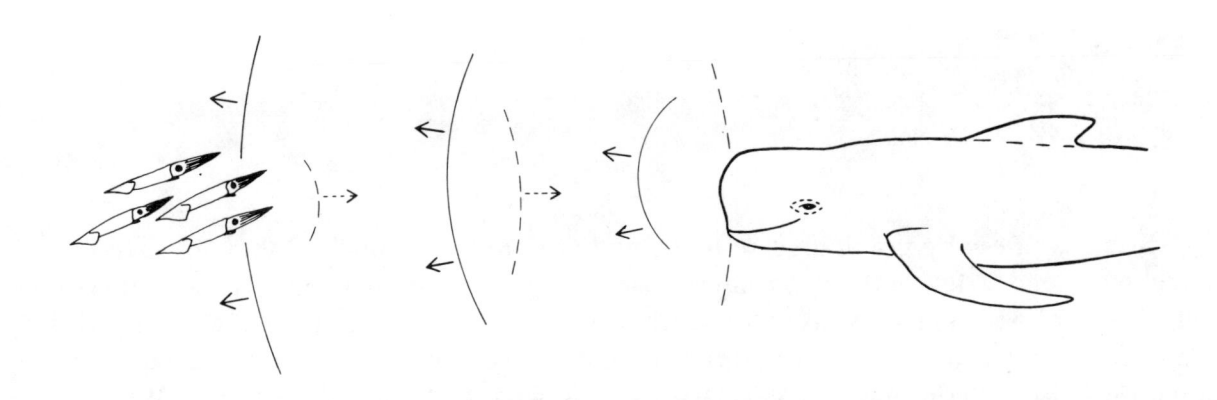

Baleen whales make sounds too! Most of these can be heard by humans. The song of the humpback whale is well known. Male humpbacks produce these songs when they are courting females. This happens only during the winter in warm tropical waters. These songs are used for social communication.

Whales make sounds at other times too. In the spring and summer while in northern waters, humpbacks don't sing, but they do produce different sounds, which are being studied. Scientists are trying to discover the meaning of these sounds. Do they tell of danger, of pain, of food? The answers are not known. There is still a good deal to learn.

Examples of whale behaviour:

Slides - Flippering, Lobtailing, Breaching

Some whales also communicate by using body motions, much as you do when you wave to a friend. A few of these movements seem to be warnings of danger. How would you tell a friend about danger if you couldn't talk? A whale might slap its tail on the water with a loud "crack". This can be heard over a long distance. But the whale could be saying something else with this motion. We can only guess what we think the message is. We don't know for sure.

ACTIVITY

Consider:

How can we use sound, rather than sight, to find something?

What you need:

a group of ten or more people
one or two different types of sound-makers for each person
a blindfold for each person

What you do:

1. Stand in a circle with the others in your class. Put on your blindfold. You will be given a sound-maker.

2. Half the group will have the same type of sound maker as you do. They will be your "pod". (This is the name for a group of whales.) The object is to find the other members of your pod. They will be making the same sound as you.

3. Walk around, making your sound. Listen for other members of your pod. As you find them, keep together. Eventually all members of your pod should be together in one group.

What you observed:

1. How was sound used to find the members of your pod? Was it easy? Was it better to repeat your sound often? Which sound worked best?

Conclusion:

1. In this activity you used sound to find the members of your pod. Explain why a pod of whales would have an easier time doing this than you did.

Summary

What you did in this activity was not echolocation. You were probably able to use sound to find the members of your pod, but if you had the ability to use echolocation, as whales do, there would not have been so much bumping and uncertainty.

Reproduction

Some whales travel great distances. You have learned that humpbacks spend their summers around Newfoundland and Labrador and their winters in the Caribbean. They don't travel just because of the weather. They go to warm tropical waters in order to reproduce. They mate one winter and the female bears a calf the next winter when the whales return to the tropics. The calf is cared for during the following year. Newborn whales are nursed with milk by their mothers much like other mammals. The milk is very rich and has a high fat content. This is well suited to a warm-blooded animal living in a cold environment. The rich milk gives the whale calf the energy it needs to survive. Humpbacks reproduce quite slowly. The females have a calf about once every two years.

People have learned about the reproduction of some whales, such as dolphins, by watching them in aquariums. Much less is known about the reproduction of whales in their natural environment.

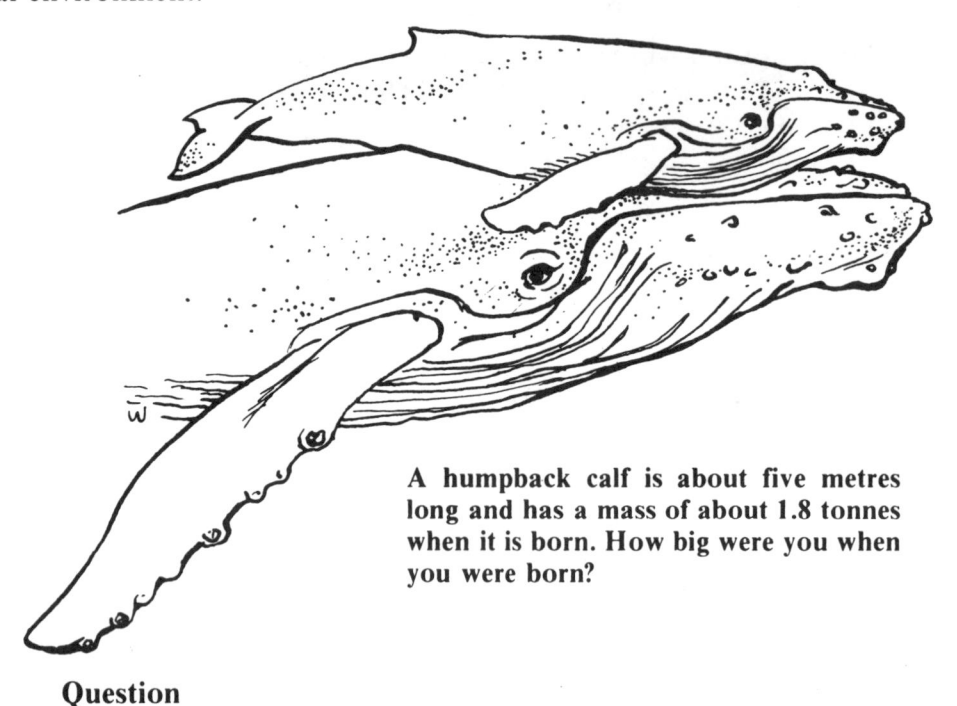

A humpback calf is about five metres long and has a mass of about 1.8 tonnes when it is born. How big were you when you were born?

Question

11. Why do humpback whales have their babies in warm water? Refer back to Activity on page 31.

NEW WORDS

adaptation
    the act of adjusting to new conditions or surroundings, a change in something produced by adapting to surroundings

baleen
    frayed, hairlike plates that some whales have instead of teeth; baleen plates hang from the whale's upper jaw and are used to strain food out of the sea water

blubber
    the thick layer of fat that whales have all around them to keep them warm and streamlined, to store food energy and help them float

buoyancy
    the ability to float

echolocation
    use of sounds for navigation and for location of food and objects

flipper
    the limbs on the side of a marine mammal; what whales have instead of arms

flukes
    the tail of a whale or dolphin

resistance
    a force that works against the motion of something; for example, a parachute works against the falling motion of a jumper

streamlined
    designed or built so that there is the least possible resistance to air or water

Lesson 5

TYPES OF WHALES

How do types of whales differ from each other?

Whales as a group of animals share a number of common adaptations. They all have smooth, streamlined bodies, a layer of blubber and a powerful horizontal tail for swimming. Whales have flippers, as forelimbs, no hind legs and the nostrils or blowhole is on top of the head. There are many different types of whales, however, and each type is adapted to its own unique niche.

Have you ever seen a minke, fin or blue whale? Look at the whales in the picture.

Question

1. *How are they similar? How are they different?*

Classification of Whales

Organisms are classified, or divided into similar groups, by their characteristics. For instance, all whales are divided into two big groups: the *toothed whales* and the *baleen whales*. These groups are sub-divided into smaller groups because of other body characteristics.

Organisms of the same kind form a *species**. For instance, all fin whales belong to the same species, whereas blue, fin and minke whales belong to three different species. Whale classification is complicated because there are 76 species of whales in the world.

Although 15 species of whales live in Newfoundland and Labrador waters, some are seen more often than others. Do you know the types of whales seen in the waters around your province? In this lesson you will learn to identify some of the species seen most commonly.

COMMON WHALES OF NEWFOUNDLAND

Pothead

Minke

Humpback

Fin

WHALES TO SCALE BASED ON SIXTEEN FOOT DORY

The poster on page 41 shows four species of whales. These are the species most commonly seen in Newfoundland and Labrador waters.

Study the diagram below and list some differences between the species. Notice the size, *dorsal fin**, tail, blow and overall shape of each whale. These are a few of the characteristics used to identify whales.

To learn how to identify different species of whales, it is important to learn what to look for. The first thing to do is to note whether the whale is small, medium or large. Because only part of the whale is seen for a short period of time, it may be difficult to estimate its size. Comparison to a nearby boat or other objects can be helpful. If you see a whale about the same size as a dory, it would be a medium-sized whale. In addition to size, the blow, dorsal fin, tail and behaviour are the most useful things to notice. A guide book about whales can help you identify species and give you more information about them.

For the rest of this lesson, we'll look at specific whales of Newfoundland and Labrador in more detail, starting with baleen whales.

COMMON WHALES OF NEWFOUNDLAND & LABRADOR

BALEEN WHALES

Humpback

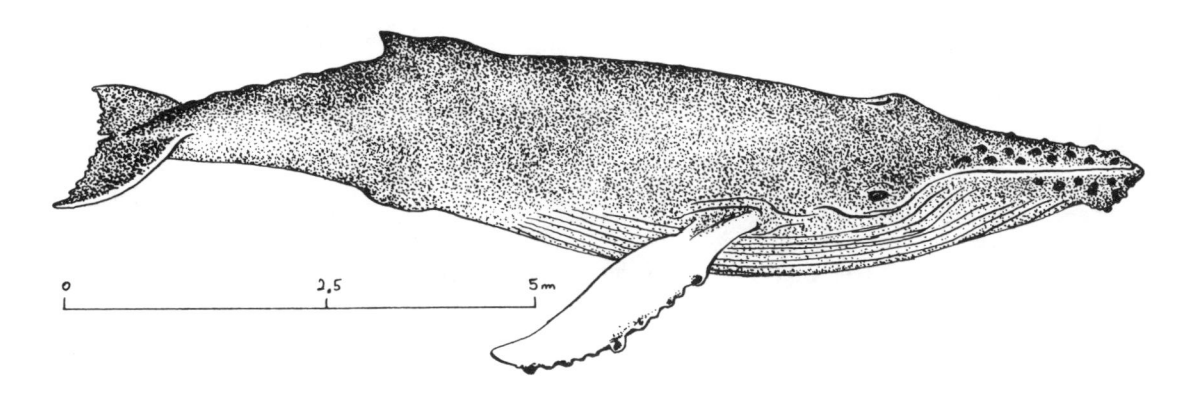

Size: large (11-14 metres, 27-36 tonnes)

Blow: balloon-shaped, usually seen before you see the whale's back

Dorsal fin: bumpy, each individual whale has a different dorsal fin

Flukes: thrown straight up in the air, exposing the undersides. Each humpback has a different pattern of black and white markings on its tail, so scientists can photograph and identify individual humpbacks.

Other Features

Humpbacks feed on capelin or krill. They are usually seen alone or in small groups. Special characteristics include knobs on the head and long white flippers. Humpbacks are well-known for their unusual behaviour such as jumping out of the water (called *breaching*) or slapping their flippers on the water.

Although they are often seen in Newfoundland and Labrador waters, humpbacks are not plentiful. There are only about 3000 humpback whales in Newfoundland and Labrador waters.

Minke (pronounced mink′ey)

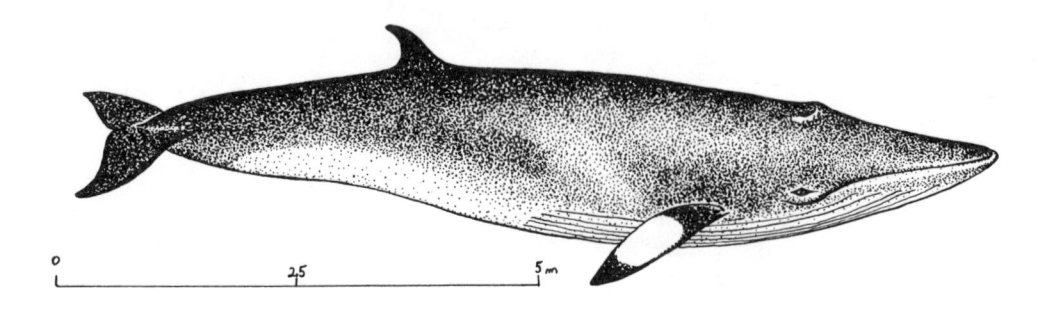

Size: medium (9 metres, 5-7 tonnes)
Blow: rarely seen
Dorsal fin: curved and pointed
Flukes: small, not lifted when diving

Other Features

Minke whales have a white band on each flipper. Sometimes these bands can be seen in the water. They are usually seen close to shore. Minkes feed on herring, capelin, squid and krill.

Local names for minke whales are *mink whales* or *herring hogs*. In some areas of the province they are also called *grampus whales*.

Minkes are the smallest of all baleen whales and are quite plentiful.

Fin

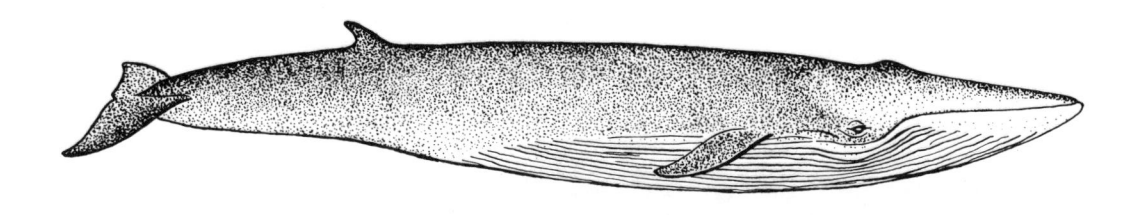

Size: large (18-23 metres, 36-45 tonnes)

Blow: tall and thin, can be seen from a great distance

Dorsal fin: small, points forward

Flukes: very large; does not usually show flukes when diving

Other Features

Fin whales are usually seen in groups of two to five. They feed on small fish and krill. Fins are very fast swimmers and can go as fast as 20 kilometres per hour. In fact, one fin whale tagged in Iceland swam 3,000 kilometres in ten days! Fin whales have one unusual characteristic; the right jaw is light in colour but the left jaw is dark. (Fin whales are also known as *finbacks* or *finners*)

Less Common Species

There are other baleen whales in Newfoundland and Labrador waters which are less common than minkes, humpbacks and fins. One is the *blue whale*.

The blue whale is the largest creature on earth. It grows to be about 25 metres long, and often weighs over 90 tonnes. A female blue whale as large as 32.5 metres and 135 tonnes has been recorded. Blue whales are sometimes seen on the west coast of Newfoundland, but in general they are rare.

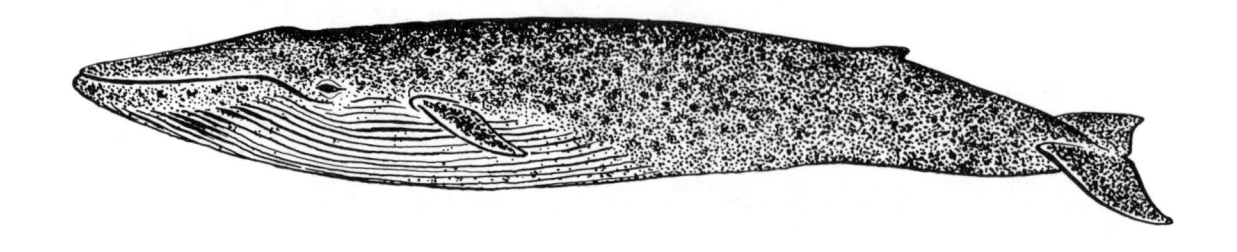

TOOTHED WHALES

Harbour Porpoise

Size: small (1.5 metres, 40 kilograms)

Blow: breathes in "puffs" every 15-20 seconds, followed by dives of three to six minutes.

Dorsal fin: broad and low

Flukes: not raised when diving

Other Features

Harbour porpoises are usually seen alone or in small groups and often stay near the surface. They eat mackerel, herring and cod. *Puffing pigs* or *puff pigs*, as harbour porpoises are often called in Newfoundland, are sometimes caught in salmon nets and codtraps.

Pothead

Size: medium (5-6 metres, 2-4 tonnes)

Blow: not seen very often

Dorsal fin: broad and low

Flukes: very small, sometimes seen on deep dives

The head is *bulbous* or shaped like a bulb

Other Features

Potheads eat mostly squid and are seen close to shore feeding from July until October. In a year when squid are plentiful around Newfoundland, you can usually see lots of potheads. They are normally seen in large groups of from five to two hundred animals. Potheads tend to stay in these groups and this can cause problems for them. Sometimes a whole group will *strand**, or beach, themselves. Although there are many possible explanations for the whales stranding, no one knows for sure what causes it. Whalers used to catch potheads quite easily by driving them ashore in places such as Dildo, Trinity Bay, where this species is commonly found.

Less Common Species

The other toothed whales which are sometimes seen around the province are killer whales and sperm whales.

Killer whales are famous. They are the whales usually seen in aquariums like the one at Stanley Park in Vancouver. They have a tall pointed dorsal fin and a white patch behind the eye. They eat squid, fish and seabirds, as well as seals and other whales.

The sperm whale is the largest of the toothed whales. It has a large, flat head and usually shows its smooth flukes when diving. Have you heard of Moby Dick? He was a sperm whale. The sperm whale feeds on squid and is found mostly in deep, offshore waters.

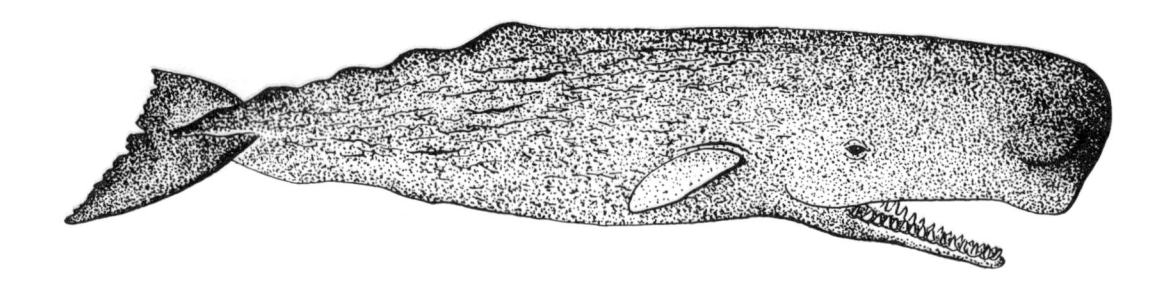

Some species of dolphins are fairly common around Newfoundland and Labrador. Dolphins normally travel in large groups and can be seen breaching and rolling.

Whale Bingo

Do you know how to play Bingo? This is a game of *Whale Bingo*. Your teacher will call out characteristics of the whales you have been learning about. Find the right one on the card below. Cover it with your marker. Call "Bingo" when you have a row completed either vertically, horizontally or diagonally.

	left jaw is dark and right jaw is light			
largest animal on earth	will sometimes become stranded on beaches	blow is rarely seen		has knobs on the head has large white flippers
large tail flukes not seen when diving	medium size usually seen alone	FREE!	large size usually seen in small groups	
		very small tail flukes sometimes seen on deep dives		medium size usually seen in large groups
small size usually seen in small groups	small tail flukes not seen when diving	bulbous head Blow is rarely seen		

Locating Whales

It is difficult to say exactly where whales can be seen. Whales move constantly and often follow their prey to new locations. From close observation of them over a period of time, however, we can predict where they are most likely to be seen. Look at the maps below. What do they tell you about where whales are commonly seen around Newfoundland and Labrador?

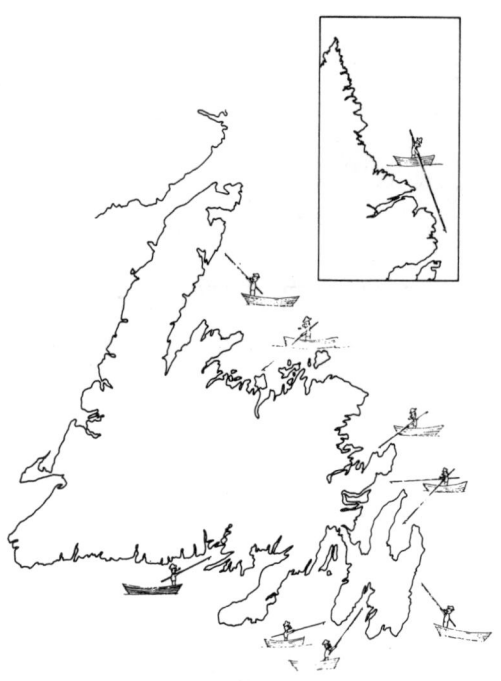

Likely Sighting Areas: Humpback Whale

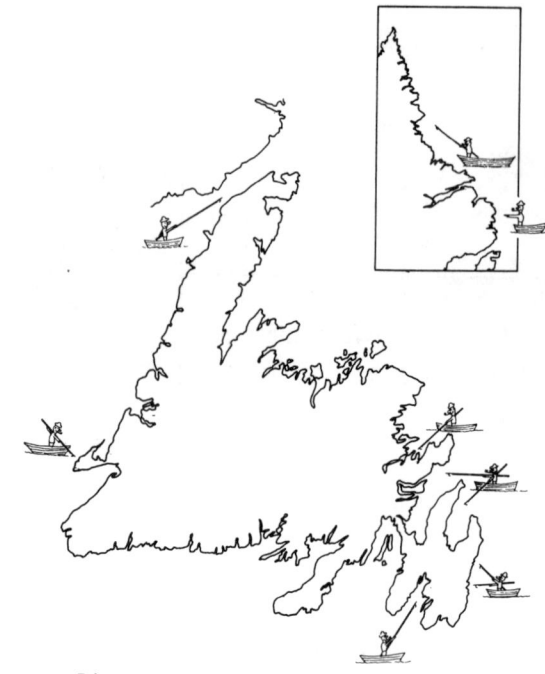

Likely Sighting Areas: Minke Whale

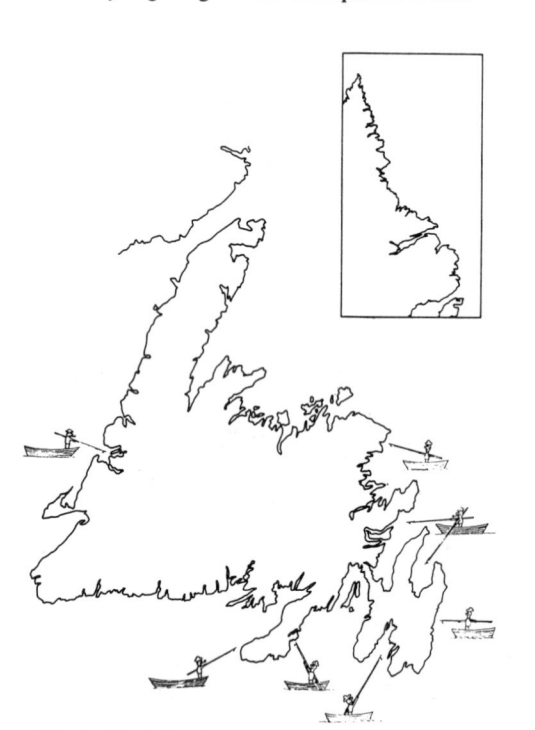

Likely Sighting Areas: Pothead Whale

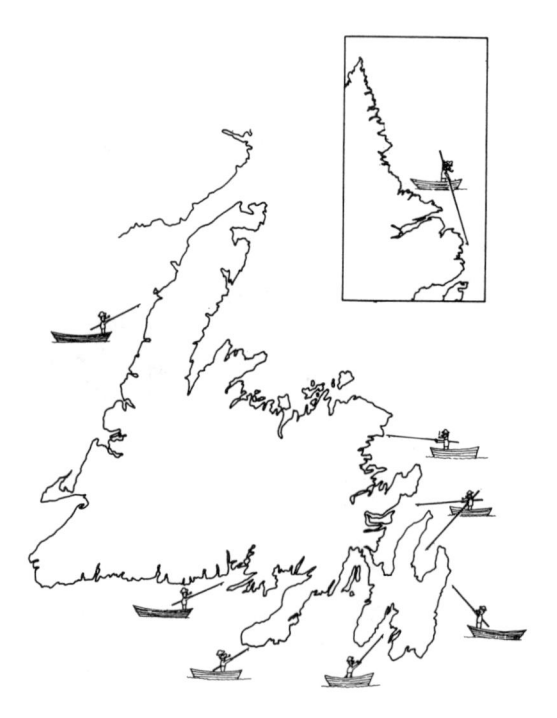

Likely Sighting Areas: Fin Whale

Questions

2. *Where are humpbacks seen most commonly? Where are potheads seen most commonly?*
3. *Find your community. Is it located near a place where whales are likely to be seen? Which species are seen the most in your area?*
4. *In what region is the highest number of whale species likely to be seen?*
5. *The maps show very few whales on the south coast of Newfoundland. Does this mean there are no whales there? Why not?*

In this lesson you have learned about some species of whales. It is not easy to identify them. Finding out the numbers of each kind of whale in a certain area is another problem. How do you think whales are counted? In the next lesson you will find out.

NEW WORDS

dorsal
   on the back

species
   a group of animals or plants that have certain characteristics in common

strand
   to leave in a helpless position: when a whale becomes stuck on a beach and is unable to get back into the water it is stranded

Lesson 6

SOME WAYS OF COUNTING ORGANISMS

How many whales were in Newfoundland and Labrador waters in 1979? How many are there now?

There are lots of whales this year!

There are not as many as last year.

Remember 1979? There were thousands of whales that year.

Is the number of whales in Newfoundland and Labrador waters increasing or decreasing? This question is not easy to answer. It is not easy to count whales.

Imagine you were given the assignment of counting the number of cats in your community. Could you possibly count every single cat? Probably not! But you could come up with an *estimate** of the number. An estimate is a guess that is based on a collection of information. You have probably used estimates in mathematics.

How would you estimate the number of cats in your community? You could go to every single house in town and find out if any cats live there. This could take a very long time. Do all cats live in people's houses?

Perhaps you could spend several hours each day for a week walking around town counting all the cats you see. The weather might affect the number of cats you would see outside. Also, one time of day might be better than another for cat-counting. Would you see all the cats in your community? How would you know you weren't counting the same cat several times?

Question

1. Can you think of another method you could use to estimate the number of cats in your community?

You can see that there are many different ways of arriving at an estimation. Each one would produce a different number. Which is right? Or rather, which is the *best estimate*? These, too, are difficult questions.

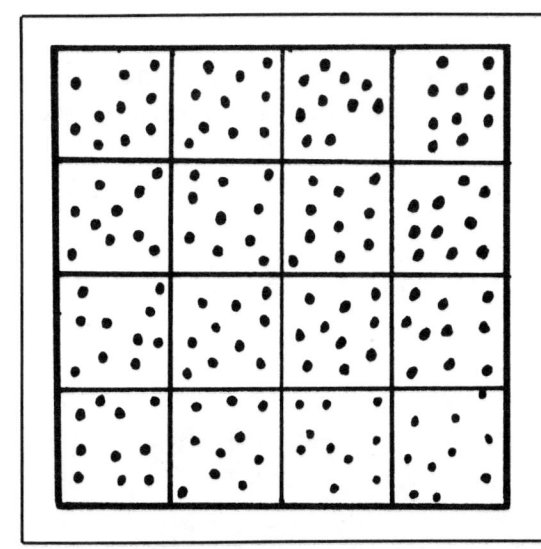

- **Something to do**

  How could you figure out the total number of dots in the large box below, as quickly as possible?

Estimating whale numbers, or *populations**, is even more difficult than estimating a cat population. Whales can be found almost anywhere in the ocean, from the Equator to the Arctic and from North America to the shores of Europe, Africa and India. They move continuously, day and night. They are only seen when they come to the surface. Breathing time can be as short as five seconds, followed by a dive that might last as long as 30 minutes. On their return to the surface, whales might be a few metres from where they breathed before, or several kilometres away in any direction. Imagine how difficult it is to count whales!

ACTIVITY

Consider:

How do you do a population survey?

What you need:

paper and pencils
an organism to survey

What to do:

1. Your teacher will tell you what organism you are to survey and what group you'll work with.
2. Meet with the other members of your group. Decide how you are going to do the survey.
3. Carry out your survey.

What you observed:

1. What method did your group use?
2. What is your group's estimate of the population? Show any mathematics you used.
3. How does your group's estimate compare with other estimates? Is it the same, larger, smaller?

Conclusions:
1. Why aren't the estimates the same?
2. Give at least two reasons for your estimate not being completely accurate.

Summary

You have seen how difficult it is to estimate a population and how much estimates can vary. This activity should make you think carefully about arguments which use estimated numbers to convince you of something. Perhaps you would want to ask what method was used to arrive at the estimate.

HOW ARE WHALES COUNTED?

There are many different methods of counting whales. Some are more modern than others. Some are more accurate than others. Often, the best method depends on the type of whale being counted.

Early Methods

During the early years of whaling, population estimates were based on the amount of time and effort needed to capture a number of whales. If capturing whales were easy and took little time, this meant there were lots of whales. On the other hand, if it took a long time to find and catch the whales, this meant there were fewer of them. This method was also used to estimate fish populations. If one year a lot of time and effort was needed to catch the fish, the population was probably low. If the next year it took less time and effort, the population was probably higher. This method is called *catch per effort** method of estimating populations.

Look at the table below. It is taken from the record of whale factories in Newfoundland and Labrador. For each year, there was about the same amount of effort used, but the number of whales caught changed.

Year	Number of Whales
1928	508
1929	382
1930	321
1931-1934	no whaling
1935	198
1936	192

Questions

2. Did the number of whales captured increase or decrease between 1928 and 1936?

3. What does that tell you about the population of whales?

4. From 1931-1934, few whales were hunted because of the depression. Why do you think the number of whales caught was still low in 1935?

This method of recording population is used for many types of animals. An important consideration is the amount of effort used.

Have you ever dug worms?

Is the amount of effort you use a factor in the number of worms you catch?

If you alone collect worms on a lawn, you will probably get a few. If five of your friends join you there will be many worms caught. There is more effort because there are more people collecting. More worms will be caught *not* because the population of worms is higher but because the effort is greater.

Think again about the early method of estimating whale populations. The number of whales caught was used to estimate the population. If it was *difficult* to catch whales, the population was thought to be low. If it was *easy,* the population was thought to be high. But effort is a factor. A high catch may have been the result of a greater effort and not because of a high population.

This method did not really give an estimate of the size of the population. Rather, it showed what was probably happening to the size of the population. Was it increasing or decreasing?

Modern Methods

Whales are still hunted today in a few areas of the world. The catch per effort method of estimating the population is still used, but it is used in combination with other methods. Even if we don't hunt whales, we still need to know how many there are. Knowing about flukes. There is a catalogue of about 3000 photographs of different whale flukes in the to understand better the role it plays in the environment we all share.

Whales can be counted individually. This can be done from boats or from airplanes. However, only the whales near or at the surface of the water can be counted. Researchers must then estimate the total number of whales based on the number which have been seen. This is not always accurate. Remember that whales spend only a small amount of time at the surface.

It's always a problem to know if the same whales are being counted over and over again. If individual whales can be recognized, it is easier to estimate the population. Photographs are now being taken to help estimate the humpback population. The flukes of each humpback whale are like a fingerprint. No two humpback whales have the same flukes. There is a catalogue of about 3000 photographs of different whale flukes seen in the northwest Atlantic. About 1500 of these humpbacks have been photographed in Newfoundland and Labrador waters. Photographs are taken regularly and compared with those in the catalogue. This helps in estimating the size of the population. If a photograph matches one in the catalogue, it means that the whale has been recorded before and is not new. If it does not match any in the catalogue, the estimated number of whales would increase.

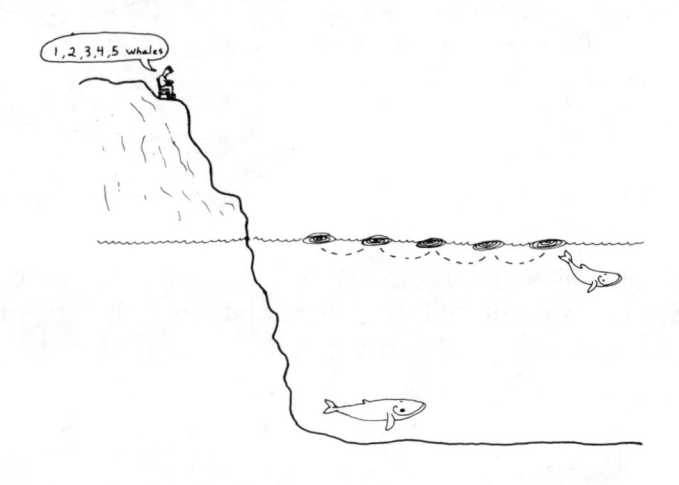

This picture is like a page from the catalogue showing the flukes of different humpbacks.

1
2
3
4
5
6

Question

5. The humpback fluke on the right was recently photographed near Newfoundland. Does this individual photo match any of the above photos? If so which one?

This match gives us two pieces of information. First, we now know this whale has already been counted. Second, we can find out where and when the first photograph was taken and learn about the movements of that whale.

A very new method for estimating whale populations is the use of whale sounds. This method is used especially with sperm whales. Tapes are made of the sounds the whales produce. It may be possible to identify individuals by the sounds they make. If so it would be possible to find out how many whales are in a group without seeing them. This is like recognizing a friend's voice on the telephone.

Whatever the method used, the estimates are always inaccurate, that is, they are not absolutely correct. We have to be very careful when looking at population estimates. When we see a new estimate, it may be that the population is actually changing or it may be that a new method for estimating is being used. Remember too that the amount of effort in surveying is also a factor.

ACTIVITY

Consider:

What makes it difficult to count whales?

What you need:

beans (or whales, whichever you can find)
counting box (one for the class)
overhead projector

What to do:

1. Your teacher will put a number of beans into the counting box and will then put the box on the overhead projector so you can see the beans on the screen.
2. Count the beans which you see through the window. Watch carefully! The beans will be moving, because your teacher will be shaking the box.

What you observed:

1. How many beans did you count?
2. How many beans do you think (or estimate) are in the box?
3. How did you arrive at that estimate?
4. Your teacher will tell you how many beans were in the box
5. How close was your estimate?

Conclusions:

1. What problems did you have in counting the beans?
2. Compare the problems of counting whales with the problems of counting beans. How are they the same? How are they different?

Summary

When you can only count what you see and you realize there are some unseen numbers, you must add to your estimate. When the organisms are moving, you may be counting the same ones several times. You must try to take away from your estimate to allow for this.

Whale Fins of Newfoundland and Labrador

It is possible to recognize some whales by their dorsal fins. The fin of each individual has a slightly different shape and may have marks or scratches. Scientists have begun developing catalogues of photographs of the dorsal fins of identified individuals, including fin whales, minkes, humpbacks and killer whales.

The photographs on this page are of the dorsal fins of humpback whales. Each is fairly distinctive. There are dorsal fins from ten different whales shown. Three of the photographs are of the same whale. Can you find those three?

SEABIRDS OF NEWFOUNDLAND AND LABRADOR

Seabirds spend most of their lives flying over the open ocean. Although they feed mainly on shellfish and fish, each group has adapted its own unique method of fishing. Gannets, for instance, plunge into the sea from great heights to catch their prey, while puffins and murres use their wings to swim underwater and chase fish.

Seabirds only return to land to breed. They are most vulnerable to disturbance during their breeding periods. The pressure of human activities such as oil development, hunting and fishing, and harassment can greatly harm seabird populations.

In Newfoundland and Labrador there are over 4 million seabirds breeding in 20 major colonies, some of which are the most important colonies in the world. Special care is needed to wisely protect our colonies for future generations to discover and appreciate.

The birds illustrated from left to right are the COMMON MURRE (Turre), the KITTIWAKE (Tickle-ace), the GANNET, and the ATLANTIC PUFFIN (Sea Parrot, Hatcherface). • Funded by Fisheries and Oceans Canada

ACTIVITY

The poster on page 59 shows four common seabirds of Newfoundland and Labrador. From left to right they are: the *Common Murre (Turr)*, the *Kittiwake (Tickle-ace)*, the *Gannet* and the *Atlantic Puffin (Sea Parrot, Hatchetface)*.

Seabirds spend much of their lives flying over open ocean. They feed mainly on fish and shellfish. Each species has developed its own unique method of fishing. Gannets, for instance, plunge into the sea from great heights to catch their prey, white puffins and murres use their wings to swim underwater and chase fish.

Seabirds always return to land to breed, usually in the spring and early summer months. In Newfoundland and Labrador there are over *four million seabirds* breeding in 20 major colonies every spring. Some of these are the most important colonies in the world.

It is when they come to land to lay their eggs that seabirds are in the most danger. They are easily upset by any disturbance during their breeding period. Human activities such as oil development, hunting and fishing, and trespassing can harm seabird populations. We must take special care to protect our important seabird colonies.

Consider:

If seabirds live most of their lives at sea how could you count them? When would you try to count them?

What to do:

Describe some methods you might use to count the seabirds in Newfoundland and Labrador. Pick one of the four common species and decide how you would estimate its population. Use your imagination.

Using Estimates

Look at the table below. It shows estimates of the population of humpback whales. The estimates were made by two different people who study whales.

Estimate of Humpback Whale Population

	World	North Atlantic Region
Estimate A	4000-6000	2000
Estimate B	under 10,000	1200

Questions

6. Why are the estimates different?

7. Can you tell from the information you have whether one is more accurate than the other?

8. What further information would you like to have before you decide which is the best estimate?

9. Ms. Jones is the editor of a magazine. She agrees with the hunting of humpbacks. Choose one of the estimates from the table and write a short letter to Ms. Jones in which you agree with her.

10. Mr. Smith disagrees with Ms. Jones. He thinks that humpbacks should not be hunted. Write a letter to Mr. Smith in which you agree with him. Use one of the estimates in your letter.

11. In writing these letters, what did you learn about using estimates?

Why Bother?

Why do people work so hard at estimating whale populations? How is the information used? From the estimates, we can compare populations today with populations of last year or several years ago. This will show if the population is changing or if it is *stable**. The estimate can be used to make a *prediction**, to suggest what may happen to the population in the future.

Population estimates are also used to determine hunting limits. If the population is estimated to be high the hunting *quota,* the number allowed to be killed, may also be high. If the estimate is low, hunting may not be allowed at all or perhaps the quota will be very low. It is important that estimates are as accurate as possible. If a quota is based on an estimate which is very far from the true number, a species may be overhunted. If the estimates are low, this may mean that the population is in danger of disappearing or becoming *extinct.* What does this mean? In the next lesson, you will learn more about this problem.

NEW WORDS

accurate
    without error, correct, exact

catch per effort
    the number caught compared to the amount of effort used in catching them

estimate
    verb, to make a guess, or to form an opinion based on incomplete information
    noun, a guess or opinion

population
    the number of individuals

prediction
    a forecast of something in the future

stable
    steady or constant, unchanging

Lesson 7

EXTINCTION IS FOREVER

Did you know that over one and one half million species of plants and animals have become extinct? Do you know what extinct means?

We say a species is *extinct** when all its members have died. When a species becomes extinct, it is gone forever. It will never be seen again. Have you ever read about dinosaurs? They are one example of species which have disappeared. Dinosaurs are extinct.

Extinction is natural. No species lives forever. Extinction usually happens when the environment changes. There are two types of extinction. One is when the species loses its original identity and changes or *evolves** into some other form. For example, the woolly mammoth evolved into the modern elephant. Today there are no woolly mammoths on earth, but the elephant has a lot of the mammoth's traits and characteristics. When animals become extinct this way, nothing of the diversity of life is lost. There are still the same number of species on earth. The animal simply changes form to adapt to the changing environment. Another kind of extinction happens when a living thing completely dies out, leaving no descendants. This type of extinction decreases the fullness and diversity of life. There is one fewer species on earth. Often this type of extinction is caused by big changes in the animals' environment. Dinosaurs disappeared suddenly and as yet no one knows for sure why they did.

Normally environmental changes are very slow. Mountains wear down and glaciers melt over many thousands of years. Plant and animal species can adapt gradually to these slow changes. Sometimes, though, changes in the environment are very quick. Fires, volcanic eruptions and floods happen naturally but very quickly. Most species cannot adapt to these changes. They don't have time. They may become extinct.

Although extinction is a natural process, the *rate* of extinction has been increasing. Many more species are becoming extinct, and it is happening much faster than ever before. The activities of humans which change the environment have been the main cause of this increase. How? Let's look at some of the activities of people which cause problems for other species.

Loss of habitat

Look at each of the pictures below.

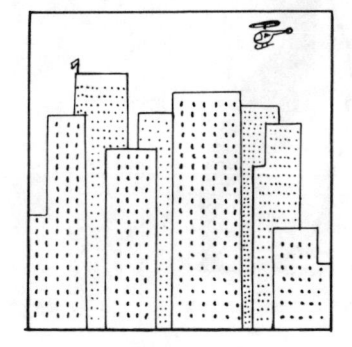

Questions

1. Tell how each picture on page 63 shows that a natural environment has been changed.
2. Suggest at least two other ways in which natural areas are being changed by humans.

Each picture shows habitats being changed or even destroyed. This happens very quickly. Some of the plants and animals which live in these areas will not survive because the changes are too fast. Does this mean that the whole species will disappear? That depends on several things. Remember that a habitat is in the area which supplies an organism's needs. This includes the need to reproduce. Sometimes, an animal species will reproduce only in one part of its habitat. If that part of the habitat is destroyed, the whole species may become extinct.

An example of a species which is threatened in this way is the whooping crane. The world population of this tall, white bird is about 80 individuals. The *only* area where it breeds is in Wood Buffalo National Park in northern Canada. If its breeding habitat were destroyed, the entire population would be wiped out!

Humans influence populations in other ways.

Overharvest

Humans kill. We kill to eat. We kill for sport and to make a living. Many years ago, clubs, spears and bows and arrows were used. Today, killing is easier. Think about the modern weapons humans use. Other animals kill too, but usually just for food. Sometimes humans kill very large numbers of animals. When we kill too many, we *overharvest**. If there is control over the number killed, as there is with caribou and moose, the species will probably survive. But if we kill too many in one year, there will not be enough to reproduce. Gradually that species will become extinct.

AUK

This bird is the great auk. At one time, there were large numbers of auks on Funk Island off the coast of Newfoundland. Look for this island on a map. The auks were killed in large numbers for food, oil and feathers. They were overharvested. In 1844, the last auk died. They will never be seen again. They are extinct.

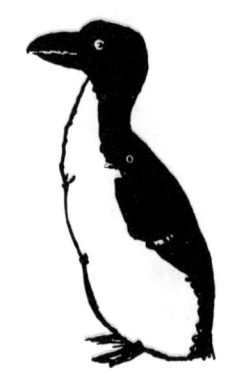

Question

3. *What would happen to the population of salmon in Newfoundland and Labrador if there were not enough left to reproduce?*

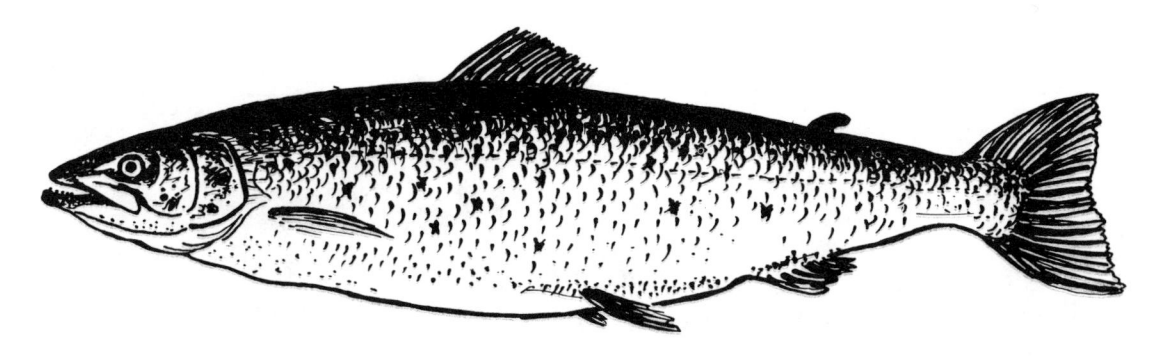

Pollution

Some of the activities of humans add poisons or *pollutants* to the environment. Are there any pollutants where you live?

Question

4. *Do you think pollutants have an effect on extinction? How?*

You have been reading about some of the ways humans speed up the process of extinction. The result is that species are lost much faster than they are replaced. Remember, extinction is natural. But what is also natural is for new species to develop. It takes a long time for new species to develop. Some of the activities of humans have increased the rate of extinction so that species are being lost faster than they are developing.

When some people hear about this, they say, "So what? What difference does it make?" These are good questions. What real difference would it make if there were no more blue whales or great auks or whooping cranes?

What difference does it make?

Human beings would be greatly affected if certain living things disappeared. Many living things provide our food. Living things supply us with products other than food, as well. Some living things are very important to the *economy* and *culture* of people.

Question

5. What would be the effect on humans if the organisms shown at right became extinct?

Question

6. What do we get from the plants and animals shown in these pictures on the left?

Question

7. What would be the effect on the people of Newfoundland and Labrador if cod became extinct?

8. What would be the effect on people in other places?

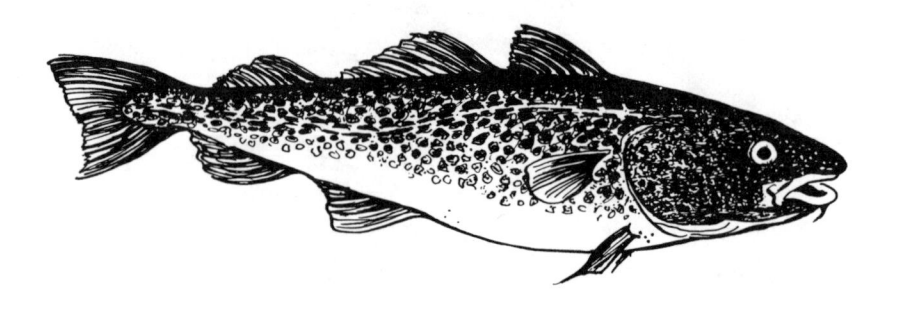

We get many useful products from living things. Most of our food and materials to make our clothes and build our homes come from living things. We get other products too. About one-third of all medicines bought at drugstores contain substances from plants, fungi and bacteria. Look at the following table. It shows where just a few of our medicines come from.

Plant	Used in Treatment of
Periwinkle plant	Cancer
Bark of coffee plant	Malaria
Snapdragon family	Heart failure
Poppy	Pain
Fungus (mold)	Infection

Fill the blanks in the table below and you will learn a few more of the vital uses of plant and animal material.

	Plant or Animal	Product
1		Bread, Cereals
2	Cotton	
3		Molasses, Sugar
4	Cacao	
5		Paper
6	Sugar Maple	
7		Cod liver oil
8		Leather

• **Something to Do**

What is your community dependent on? List all the food that is produced in your area. Make a separate list of some food that is brought to your local stores from other parts of the world.

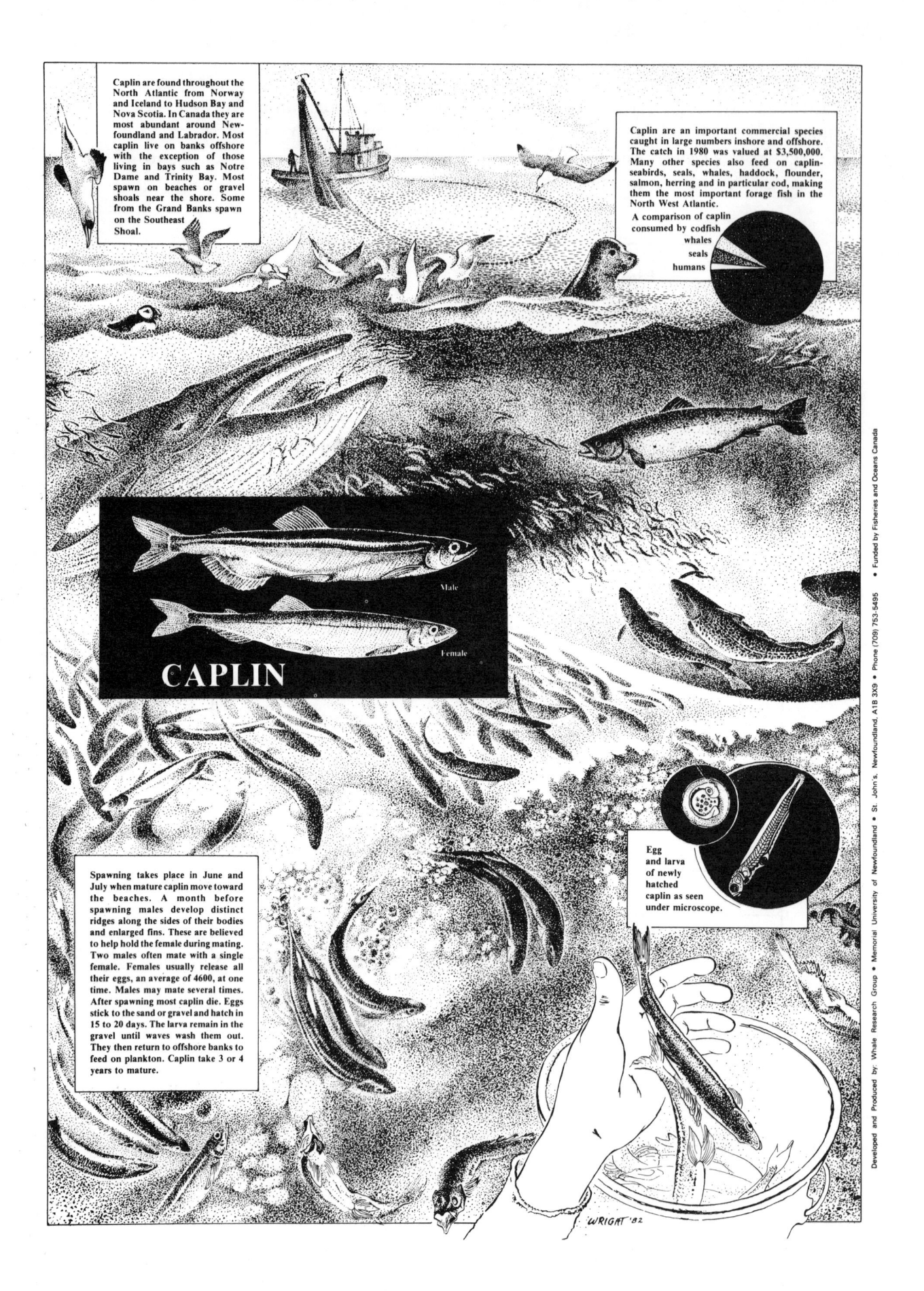

Caplin are found throughout the North Atlantic from Norway and Iceland to Hudson Bay and Nova Scotia. In Canada they are most abundant around Newfoundland and Labrador. Most caplin live on banks offshore with the exception of those living in bays such as Notre Dame and Trinity Bay. Most spawn on beaches or gravel shoals near the shore. Some from the Grand Banks spawn on the Southeast Shoal.

Caplin are an important commercial species caught in large numbers inshore and offshore. The catch in 1980 was valued at $3,500,000. Many other species also feed on caplin-seabirds, seals, whales, haddock, flounder, salmon, herring and in particular cod, making them the most important forage fish in the North West Atlantic.

A comparison of caplin consumed by codfish whales seals humans

CAPLIN

Male
Female

Egg and larva of newly hatched caplin as seen under microscope.

Spawning takes place in June and July when mature caplin move toward the beaches. A month before spawning males develop distinct ridges along the sides of their bodies and enlarged fins. These are believed to help hold the female during mating. Two males often mate with a single female. Females usually release all their eggs, an average of 4600, at one time. Males may mate several times. After spawning most caplin die. Eggs stick to the sand or gravel and hatch in 15 to 20 days. The larva remain in the gravel until waves wash them out. They then return to offshore banks to feed on plankton. Caplin take 3 or 4 years to mature.

WRIGHT '82

Developed and Produced by: Whale Research Group • Memorial University of Newfoundland • St. John's, Newfoundland, A1B 3X9 • Phone (709) 753-5495 • Funded by Fisheries and Oceans Canada

Extinction Affects the Environment

As you know, each and every animal and plant species has a special role to play in the natural environment. If an animal or plant becomes extinct, what effect does this have on the rest of the environment? Think back to what happened in the Web of Life game you played in Lesson 3. When players stepped out of the circle or let go of their strings, was anyone else affected? Sometimes we don't know how important an organism is until it's gone. Then it's too late.

Look at the food web below. Imagine what would happen to the other organisms if capelin disappeared.

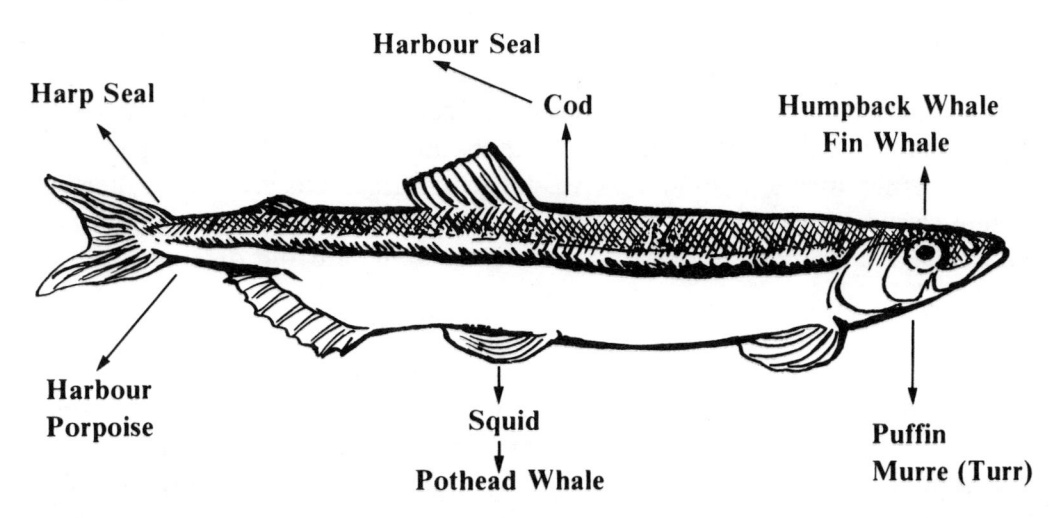

Harp Seal
Harbour Seal
Cod
Humpback Whale
Fin Whale
Harbour Porpoise
Squid
Pothead Whale
Puffin
Murre (Turr)

Questions

9. What would happen to the cod, squid and puffin populations if capelin were gone?
10. Would the seals and whales be affected? How?
11. How would you be affected?

You have thought about what would happen if just one key species were to become extinct. We know that the extinction of capelin would affect a large number of other organisms. We know much less about whales. We don't know for sure what would happen to the ocean if whales became extinct. It may be serious or it may have only a minor effect. Is it worth the chance?

Do you have a bicycle? What would happen to the wheel if you removed one spoke? It probably wouldn't make much difference. If you took away a second spoke or a third, it may not make much difference, either. But if you keep removing spokes, at some point you will remove one, just one, which will cause the wheel to collapse.

Losing a spoke from the wheel is like losing a species from the planet. The loss of just one spoke or one species may not be noticed. But the lost species, like the lost spokes, add up. At some time the loss of one species, like the loss of one spoke will be very important to life on earth. We don't know which spoke or which species will be the important one.

How important are humans?

Human beings are only one of a large variety of living species on our planet. We are fairly new on the scene. Many other species have been on earth much longer than we have. But some humans feel that we are the most important species and that we have the right to decide which other species should survive. Do you agree? Do you think that we have a greater right to survive than other species? Do we have the right to destroy other species for our own gains? These questions have produced much debate and disagreement. What do you think?

How do humans help?

Some of the activities of humans prevent extinction. We have hunting regulations to protect animals from overharvest. In Newfoundland and Labrador, there are two government acts — The Ecological Reserves Act and the Environmental Assessment Act. These acts have given us rules to protect the environment. We have provincial parks and two large national parks. We have other special *sanctuaries** where hunting is not allowed. Have you ever been to Cape St. Mary's, or Witless Bay Seabird Sanctuaries, or to Salmonier Nature Park? These are examples of ways people are trying to help prevent extinction. Can you think of other ways?

Humans also help by giving special protection to species which are almost extinct. For example, the blue whale and the humpback whale are described as *endangered* species. This means that they are in danger of becoming extinct, partly because of the activities of humans. They are endangered because they were overharvested, during the whaling days. They are now given special protection.

ACTIVITY

Consider:
How does a species survive?

What you need:
A group of 10-15 people (the class may be divided into two groups)
A large number of small stones

What to do:
1. The members of the group should sit in a circle. Each person represents a different species living in the same environment as the other species represented in the circle.

2. The teacher will put some stones under the waste basket in the centre of the circle. They represent *food* which all species need to survive. You will not know how many stones are there.
3. The object is to collect enough food so that your species will survive. This happens when you have collected ten *food stones*. Each person or species has a turn feeding and has a choice of how much food to take. You can take none (this doesn't mean you will starve), one, two or three food stones. After every species has a turn feeding, the teacher will double the number of stones left in the centre. Everyone has a turn again. This is repeated several times. When one species has collected ten food stones, the game ends. That species has survived. The others become extinct.

What you observed:
1. What things other than food are needed for your species to survive?
2. Would one species survive if all the other species were extinct?

Conclusions:
1. Pretend you have a friend, Alice, who is ill and was not in school today. She is very interested in this game. Write a letter to her. Describe how all the species in your group worked together so that one could survive.

Summary

The activities of organisms living together in the environment must balance one another. This activity as well as your reading of this lesson should show you that co-operation is necessary. One organism cannot survive alone.

Whaling

Because of their large size, whales can produce large amounts of oil, meat and other useful items. As soon as people invented boats, a primitive form of whaling started. The Inuit and other native people began hunting whales by harpoon from their kayaks and canoes hundreds of years ago.

A whale fishery began as early as the tenth century off the French and Spanish coasts and was well set up by the twelfth century. The Spanish started sailing all the way to the banks of Newfoundland in the 1500s to hunt whales. By the 1600s English, Basque, Dutch, Spanish and German ships were all sailing to the Arctic in search of whales. Heavy, wooden boats were used even after iron boats were invented because the wood could withstand the pressure of the ice floes. By the middle of the nineteenth century, harpoon guns were used, as well as hand harpoons.

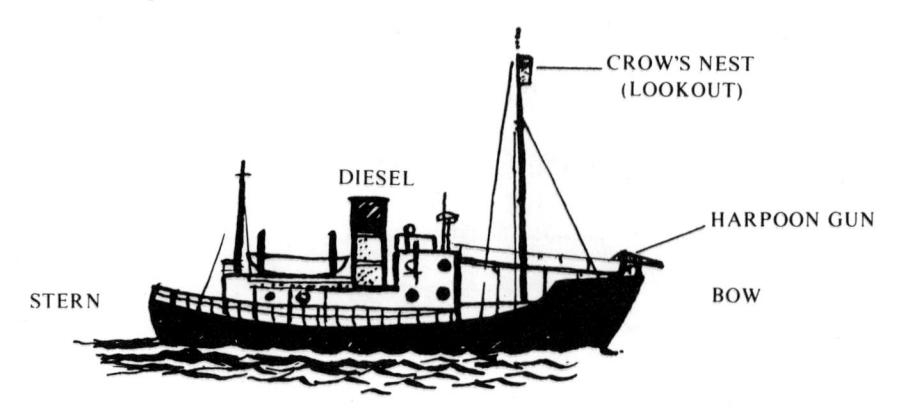

Around 1900, the Newfoundland Whaling Company was formed. By 1905, there were 18 whaling stations in operation around the province. The whaling ships moved fast and were able to chase whales easily. Exploding harpoons were used to kill the whales. They were shot from the ship into the whale. Shortly after, the harpoon exploded inside the whale, usually killing it instantly. The large, slower-moving baleen whales, such as blues and humpbacks, were most easily caught.

With all this hunting, the number of whales in Newfoundland and Labrador quickly decreased.

By 1950, there were only three active whaling factories in Newfoundland at Williamsport (White Bay), at Hawke's Harbour (Labrador) and at Dildo (Trinity Bay). Can you find these communities on a map?

Through the 1950s, the larger whales were becoming scarce. Hunters began taking smaller whales, such as potheads and minkes. Whale *drives* were not uncommon. Potheads, which tend to be found in large groups, were herded together and driven into shore and killed.

The number of whales continued to decrease. In the 1960s, the International Whaling Commission set strict *quotas** on the number of whales which could be taken at Newfoundland whaling stations.

Many people were very concerned over the small number of large whales left in the ocean. Several countries decided to stop whaling. In 1972, Canada banned commercial whaling. This meant that whales could not be killed for the sale of the products. Native people in northern Canada are still allowed to kill small numbers of whales. They use the products for themselves and not for sale.

In some countries some species of whales which are not scarce are still hunted. Japan, Brazil, Norway and the U.S.S.R. are examples. However, *quotas* are set on each species and there is no hunting of any species which is endangered.

The purpose of the ban on whaling was to allow whale numbers to increase. It's difficult to know whether the whale populations are increasing now that whaling is banned here. You already know how hard it is to estimate whale populations!

The humpback whale is an interesting example. Why is it considered endangered? Humpbacks can be seen quite easily off Newfoundland in summer. But on a world-wide scale, the size of the population is small, only a few thousand. Many of these feed on capelin in Newfoundland waters. The ones we see here make up a large portion of the world population. We can see them easily but in other places of the world they are very, very rare.

Humpbacks *seem* to be increasing. Certainly we hear much more about them. Is this because there are more of them? Or is it because we are more aware of them? In Newfoundland, a problem has developed. Humpbacks are causing damage to fishing gear. As a result, we hear more about them and the conflict with the fishermen. What is the nature of this conflict?

NEW WORDS

evolve
> when a species develops or changes from one form of itself to a new form, in order to adapt to environmental changes

extinct species
> all members dead, not a single living member on earth

overharvest
> kill too many organisms so the population becomes scarce

quota
> an allowable amount of the total catch that can be taken by each country and is specified by law; for example, in 1978 the Portuguese were given a quota of 10,000 tonnes of cod to be caught off Newfoundland: The Canadian Federal Department of Fisheries and Oceans set the quota

sanctuary
> a place where species are protected

Lesson 8

A CONFLICT

How does man come in conflict with other species in using the planet's natural resources?

Should Whales be Protected?

There are many good reasons to protect animals from extinction due to man's activity. There are also problems to be solved and expenses to be paid.

Not everyone feels that whales should be protected in Newfoundland and Labrador. Fishermen have many complaints about whales damaging their fishing gear, especially cod traps. Sometimes gill nets are damaged too. The chart, "Common Fishing Gear in Newfoundland and Labrador", page 77, shows the different types of gear. A fisherman's gear is the tool he uses to earn his living.

Fish become caught in fishing gear because the gear is hard to see in the water. Whales feeding inshore are busy and sometimes they don't see the gear in time to avoid a *collision**. Sometimes whales swim right through the gear leaving a big hole that is expensive to mend. Other times whales may get tangled up in the gear and become *entrapped**. When this happens, there is usually greater damage to the gear. The fisherman cannot fish until the whale is released or escapes and his gear's mended. The lost fishing time costs the fisherman a lot of money. Getting caught in fishing gear is a serious problem for whales too. If they are badly tangled up, they might drown.

Articles about whales have often appeared in local newspapers. The article on the next page was in the *Evening Telegram* on January 26, 1980. Read it carefully and then answer the questions which follow.

Questions

1. *How much damage was done to fishing gear by whales in 1979?* (Answer in dollars).
2. *In what other way, besides gear loss, did fishermen lose money because of whale collisions?*
3. *Why do whales collide with fishing gear?*
4. *Which type of whale is involved in most collisions?*
5. *Why has the number of collisions increased over the last five years?*
6. *Give two reasons why more whales are seen inshore now than several years ago.*
7. *Would it help solve the problem if whaling were allowed again in Newfoundland? Why or why not?*
8. *Does the shooting of whales help? Why or why not?*
9. *Is is easier to remove a dead whale or a live whale from gear? Why?*
10. *How can collisions be prevented?*

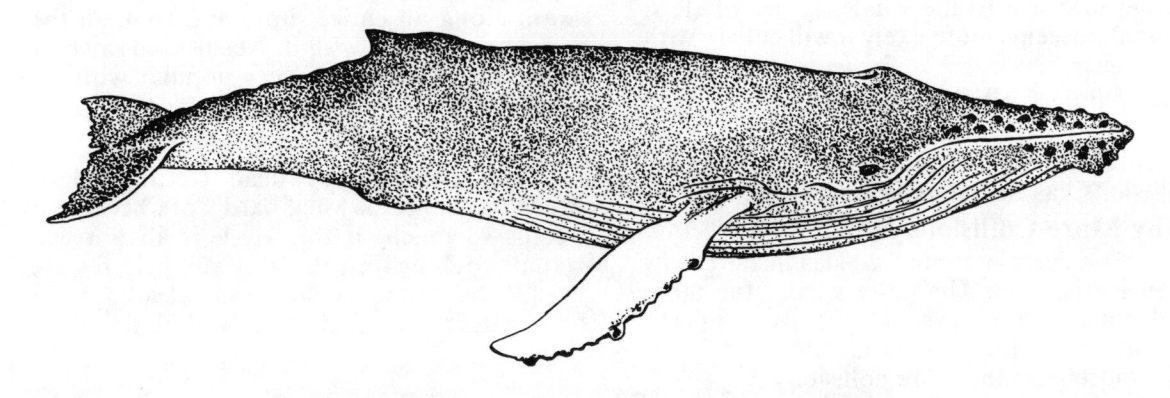

IT'S A BATTLE FOR EXISTENCE
By The Whale Research Group

Last year we wrote several articles for the *Evening Telegram* describing the trouble Newfoundland's inshore fishermen were having with whales. The purpose of this article is to answer questions frequently asked about the problem.

How Big is the Problem?

Whale collisions with fishing gear in 1979 resulted in $250,000 in gear loss and damages. Each of these collisions also resulted in lost time fishing during the brief period the inshore fisherman has to earn his living. These downtime losses are in excess of $1 million.

Where is the Problem Worst?

Damage to cod traps is worst in St. Mary's Bay and on the southern shore of the Avalon Peninsula. Gill net damage is worst on the northeast coast usually in Trinity and Bonavista Bays. Much of the damage to salmon nets, such as on the south coast, is caused by basking sharks. Some years, damage is serious in southern Labrador.

Why do Whales Collide with Gear?

Bait, mostly caplin, causes fishermen and whales to fish in the same inshore areas. The bait which attracts whales, also attracts the fish which, in turn, attracts the fishermen. Thus whales tend to be thickest in the good fishing areas.

Do all Whales have Collisions?

Yes. In 1979, humpbacks, fins, minkes, potheads, and belugas, as well as several kinds of porpoises were known to collide with fishing gear. Most collisons involve the humpback. The next most accident-prone is the minke, and next to that the fin whale. In general it is the baleen whales which feed on very small bait that collide with gear rather than the toothed whales that feed on larger fish.

How do Collisions Affect Whales?

Most collisions do more damage to the fishermen's gear and livelihood than to the whale. However some collisions cause injury and even death to the whale. If the whale is injured, it seems more likely it will collide with more gear.

Are Whale Collisions Increasing?

Yes? Over the past five years the number of collisions per year and the cost of those collisions has increased dramatically.

Why More Collisions Now?

First there are more whales inshore now than in the past. The more whales the more collisions. Second, over the past five years the amount of fishing gear in the water has tripled. The more gear the more collisions.

How can Fishermen be Helped?

The best solution for helping fishermen is to prevent the collisions in the first place.

Can Collisions be Prevented?

Yes, we think so. The basic idea is to make fishing gear easier for whales to detect. This is best done by using sound devices on nets. These sound devices must be designed so that fish cannot hear them but whales can.

Why are More Whales Inshore?

Whales may have been forced inshore because of a shortage of caplin on the offshore banks. Caplin is the major food of whales. A second reason for the increased number of whales inshore may be an actual increase in the population size of some species. Most whales were hunted dangerously close to extinction earlier in this century. A discontinuation of whaling since 1972 in Canada has given the whales a chance to increase their numbers.

Would Whaling Help?

Probably not. Whales have moved inshore to try and find more caplin. Fisheries and Oceans Canada has stopped the offshore caplin fishery and this, in time, should help increase the number of caplin and move the whales offshore. The International Whaling Commission which is in charge of whaling laws would never agree to a whaling program designed to reduce the numbers to previous dangerous lows. Also the humpback is an endangered species now so it would be impossible to hunt it, and it is the whale that does 70% of all the gear damage. Finally, the number of whales being killed by collisions is already high. This has not affected collisions; neither would whaling.

What is the Effect of Shooting?

Whale shooting is dangerous. It's unlikely that shooting a whale kills it but it does injure it and cause it pain. Injured whales do more damage to gear than uninjured whales. In one case, a man shot a whale and it went berserk. It swam along an entire shore and took all the communities' nets with it. Needless to say that whale shooter was not very popular with his neighbours.

Is it Difficult to Free a Whale?

Yes, if the whale is dead. Getting a dead whale out of gear is long, hard work because it weighs so much. If the whale is alive it will actually pull against the gear and help release itself. The sooner a whale is released from fishing gear the less damage will be done.

COMMON INSHORE FISHING GEAR OF NEWFOUNDLAND AND LABRADOR

JIGGER
A traditional lead jigger or a stainless steel Norweigian jigger is used — no bait is needed. It is lowered almost to the bottom and then drawn up and down. Cod are attracted and may be caught by the head, body or tail.

SALMON NET
Salmon nets are made of nylon with many small floats along the head and a lead foot rope. Large buoys keep the net on the surface and heavy anchors hold it in place. Salmon are caught by their gills and removed without hauling the net from the water. Nets are 50 fathoms long.

HANDLINE
The hook is usually baited with squid. At times a series of hooks with artificial bait is also attached to the line. A heavy lead weight keeps the bait near the bottom. Fishermen often tend a line on each side of the boat.

COD TRAP
A cod trap is a mesh box with a floor which rests on the bottom. The top is suspended by many small floats and large buoys at the corners, sides and back. Each of these is moored by a heavy anchor. As cod fish follow capelin, they are diverted into the door of the trap by the leader which extends from the door toward shore. Traps vary in size and shape, an average being 60 fathoms in the round and 12 fathoms deep with a 50 fathom leader. Traps are usually hauled twice a day by a crew working from a trap boat assisted by a dory. The door is closed first by hauling up a rope attached to the bottom front. Then the front corners are hauled up and the fish are gradually concentrated along one side or back by hauling in the mesh bottom. The catch is removed to the boat by a dip net.

Drawings are NOT to scale.

1 fathom = 6 feet = 1.83 metres

GILL NETS (for ground fish)
Gill nets, made of monofilament, are similar in construction to salmon nets. They are sunk to the bottom by small weights. The ends are marked by buoys. Nets are hauled into the boat to remove fish, then reset. Often three or four nets are joined together. Nets are 50 fathoms long and 1 fathom deep.

TRAWLS (Long Lines)
Trawls have many short lines attached at regular intervals. Each short line has a hook which is usually baited with squid. Trawls are set on the bottom with a small anchor at each end and marked by buoys. They are hauled to the boat to remove the fish and usually coiled in tubs to be rebaited ashore. Each line is 50 fathoms long and 20 to 30 lines are often set together.

WRIGHT '82

Developed and Produced by: Whale Research Group • Memorial University of Newfoundland • St. John's, Newfoundland, A1B 3X9 • Phone (709) 753-5495 • Funded by Fisheries and Oceans Canada

The whale research group at Memorial University has shown many fishermen how to release entrapped whales on their own. It is a definite advantage to the fishermen to free a trapped whale as quickly as possible, so he can repair his nets and get back to fishing. Of course, being freed by the fisherman is also to the whale's advantage! By 1983, many men were taking an active role in freeing whales and keeping the gear damage to a minimum.

Mr. Ellison Barfett of Salvage, Newfoundland is one fisherman who has had a lot of experience with whales. In 1979, he was forced to stop cod fishing because 50 of his gill nets were destroyed. The nets alone cost him $7,500.00. Lost time and lost fish cost him even more money. Yet Mr. Barfett saved seven humpbacks that year in Bonavista Bay!

"I've broken in horses and ranch cattle, so I know about big animals and they don't frighten me," says Mr. Barfett. "Like a bad horse in trouble, a trapped whale seems to calm down. I believe it knows you are trying to help."

Year	Number of Entrapped Humpback Whales
1979	47
1980	61
1981	31
1982	35
1983	35

Questions

11. *Did the number of entrapped humpback whales increase or decrease from 1980 to 1981? By how much?*
12. *Why do you think the 1980 figure for entrapped humpbacks was the highest?*

Sharks and Jaws

Not all of the large creatures in the ocean are whales! Other animals, besides whales, cause damage to fishermen's gear and the basking shark is one of them. Basking sharks are often confused with whales because of their large size. A major difference is that a shark is a *fish* and a whale, as you know, is a *mammal*.

Basking sharks, unlike most other sharks, have jaws that contain very small, dull teeth. They feed on plankton (red bait). Basking sharks are the second largest fish in the world. Only the *whale shark* is bigger. A mature basking shark can be over 10 metres long and weigh nearly 4,000 kilograms.

Fossils tell us that sharks have existed since the time of the dinosaurs. They are very old creatures, indeed. Unfortunately, we know very little about the life of the basking shark. We do not even know for sure how a mother shark gives birth or how many babies she has.

One bright spot in all these problems is that basking sharks are worth money. If a fisherman sells part of a basking shark which was caught in his gear, he can get some money to help pay for his damages. The value of basking sharks is due to their huge livers, which are sold locally and made into oil. The oil is used on machinery and in making comestics, like mascara for eyelashes. One basking shark may have 1,000 kilograms of liver in its belly. The many fins of the shark are also sold and dried. Then they are shipped to China and Hong Kong and used in shark fin soup. Researchers are working to find uses for the hides, flesh, stomach contents and cartilage of this gigantic shark. Perhaps markets for these shark parts will develop in the future. If fishermen could sell most of the shark locally they could recover more than the cost of their damaged gear.

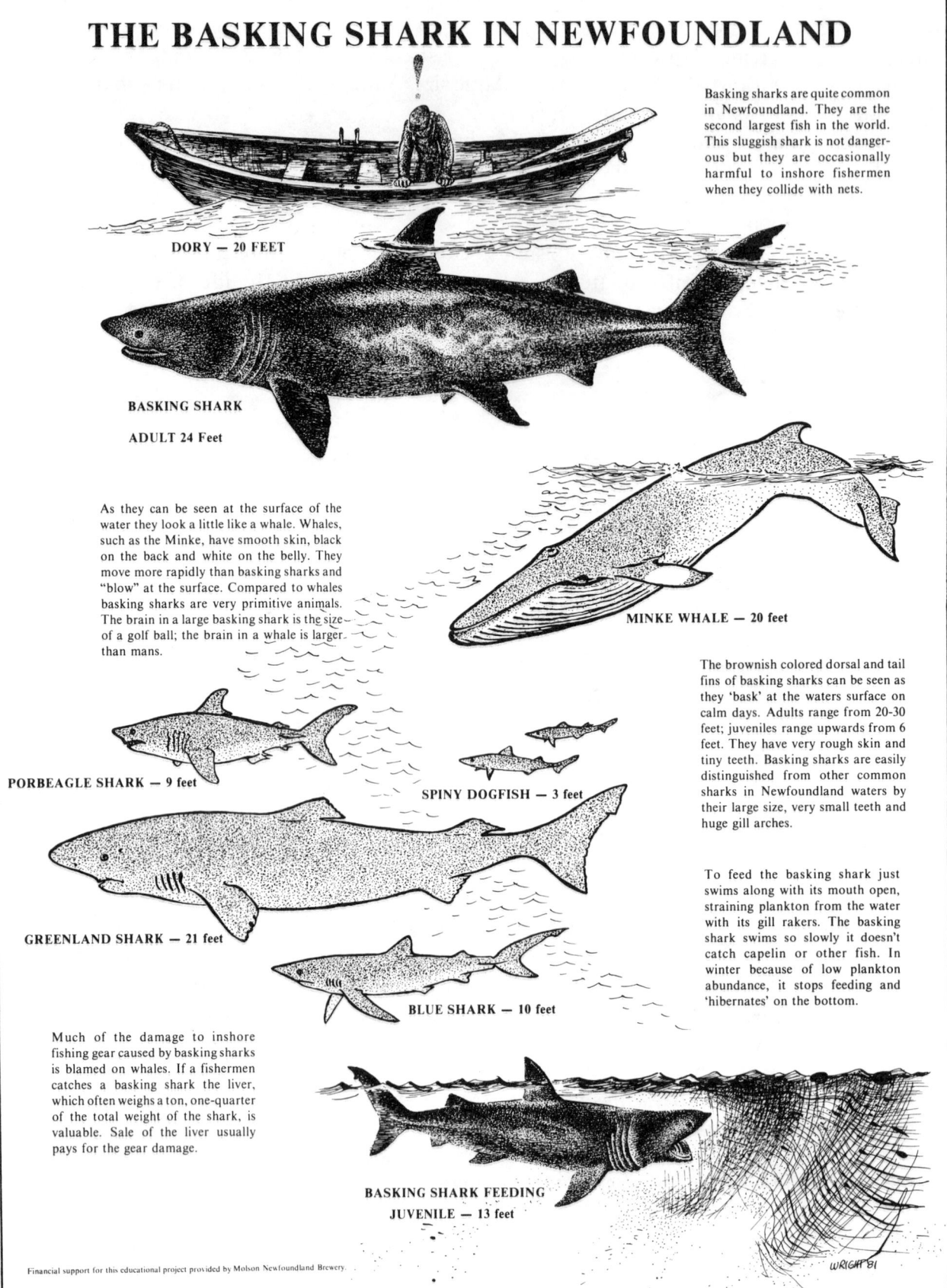

THE BASKING SHARK IN NEWFOUNDLAND

Basking sharks are quite common in Newfoundland. They are the second largest fish in the world. This sluggish shark is not dangerous but they are occasionally harmful to inshore fishermen when they collide with nets.

DORY — 20 FEET

BASKING SHARK
ADULT 24 Feet

As they can be seen at the surface of the water they look a little like a whale. Whales, such as the Minke, have smooth skin, black on the back and white on the belly. They move more rapidly than basking sharks and "blow" at the surface. Compared to whales basking sharks are very primitive animals. The brain in a large basking shark is the size of a golf ball; the brain in a whale is larger than mans.

MINKE WHALE — 20 feet

The brownish colored dorsal and tail fins of basking sharks can be seen as they 'bask' at the waters surface on calm days. Adults range from 20-30 feet; juveniles range upwards from 6 feet. They have very rough skin and tiny teeth. Basking sharks are easily distinguished from other common sharks in Newfoundland waters by their large size, very small teeth and huge gill arches.

PORBEAGLE SHARK — 9 feet

SPINY DOGFISH — 3 feet

To feed the basking shark just swims along with its mouth open, straining plankton from the water with its gill rakers. The basking shark swims so slowly it doesn't catch capelin or other fish. In winter because of low plankton abundance, it stops feeding and 'hibernates' on the bottom.

GREENLAND SHARK — 21 feet

BLUE SHARK — 10 feet

Much of the damage to inshore fishing gear caused by basking sharks is blamed on whales. If a fishermen catches a basking shark the liver, which often weighs a ton, one-quarter of the total weight of the shark, is valuable. Sale of the liver usually pays for the gear damage.

BASKING SHARK FEEDING
JUVENILE — 13 feet

WRIGHT '81

Financial support for this educational project provided by Molson Newfoundland Brewery.

Developed and Produced by: Whale Research Group • Memorial University of Newfoundland • St. John's, Newfoundland, A1B 3X9 • Phone (709) 753-5495 • Funded by Fisheries and Oceans Canada

What does this damage mean to fishermen? Many are angry and upset. You might be, too, if you lost thousands of dollars worth of gear and fishing time. Would you want to protect whales and increase their numbers if you were losing money because of them?

Sometimes fishermen express their opinions when they report damage. Here are some of their comments.

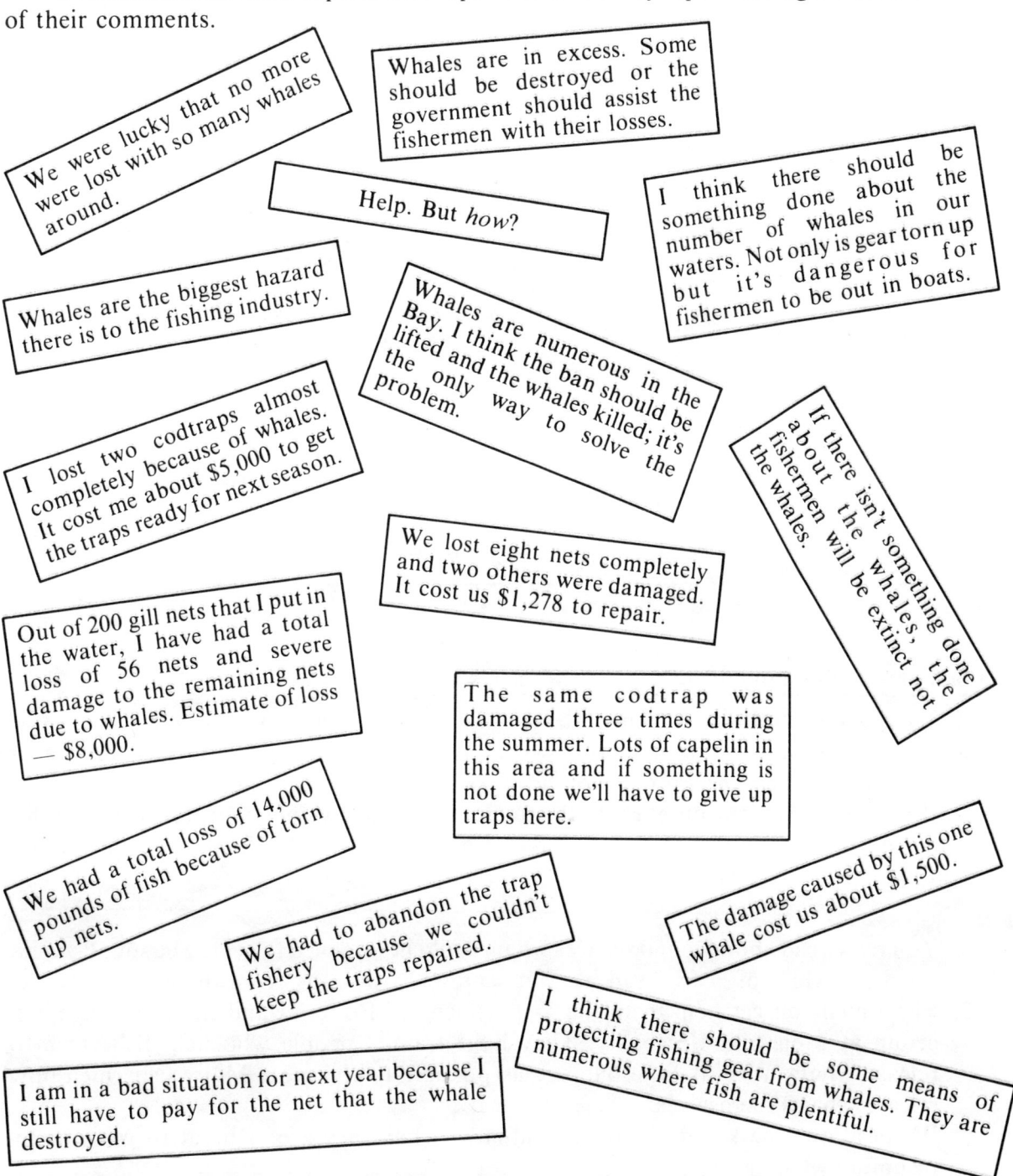

We were lucky that no more were lost with so many whales around.

Whales are in excess. Some should be destroyed or the government should assist the fishermen with their losses.

Help. But *how*?

I think there should be something done about the number of whales in our waters. Not only is gear torn up but it's dangerous for fishermen to be out in boats.

Whales are the biggest hazard there is to the fishing industry.

Whales are numerous in the Bay. I think the ban should be lifted and the whales killed; it's the only way to solve the problem.

If there isn't something done about the whales, the fishermen will be extinct not the whales.

I lost two codtraps almost completely because of whales. It cost me about $5,000 to get the traps ready for next season.

We lost eight nets completely and two others were damaged. It cost us $1,278 to repair.

Out of 200 gill nets that I put in the water, I have had a total loss of 56 nets and severe damage to the remaining nets due to whales. Estimate of loss — $8,000.

The same codtrap was damaged three times during the summer. Lots of capelin in this area and if something is not done we'll have to give up traps here.

We had a total loss of 14,000 pounds of fish because of torn up nets.

We had to abandon the trap fishery because we couldn't keep the traps repaired.

The damage caused by this one whale cost us about $1,500.

I am in a bad situation for next year because I still have to pay for the net that the whale destroyed.

I think there should be some means of protecting fishing gear from whales. They are numerous where fish are plentiful.

Often the angry comments of fishermen are reported in newspapers and on television. It sometimes seems as though all fishermen hate whales. This is very far from the truth. Most fishermen have a great respect for whales. Unfortunately, newspapers do not usually report the ways in which many fishermen help entrapped whales.

This is an example of the damage report fishermen complete.

```
WHALE DAMAGE TO FISHING GEAR REPORT
— Retain this card until needed —
Name: THOMAS CORCORAN  Address: RIVERHEAD, St. MARY'S BAY
Phone: 525-2688  Date damage occurred: June 25, 1983
Location of damaged gear: St. Vincents Bay, S.M.B.
Type of gear: Gill Nets          Depth of water: 16 Fms
Do you think the collision occurred at night ☒  or during the day ☐
Describe the nature and extent of damage: 2 Gillnets: lost Buoys and Moorings, 4 Gillnets destroyed beyond repairs

Estimate cost of repairs: $1,045.00
Estimate days lost fishing: 18 days
Estimate daily yield of fish taken in this gear: 1,200 lbs
Was the animal caught in the gear?  ☒ alive  ☐ dead  Kind (if known) _____
Comments: This animal was caught in nets and got away with some of the nets around it.

Please fill in and mail this card as soon as possible after the gear damage has happened. Thank you for your cooperation.
```

What can be done to cut down on fishermen's losses?

There are several ways in which the problem of collisions can be minimized. As you read each of these suggestions decide whether it would help to *prevent* a collision or whether it would help *after* a collision has taken place. Number your paper from one to nine. Put a "P" beside the numbers of the suggestions which would help prevent collisions; put an "A" beside the numbers of the suggestions which would help after a collision has taken place.

1. You have read about sound devices which could be attached to gear. The sound would warn the whale of gear ahead but not scare the fish away from the gear.
2. Fishermen can get help from the Department of Fisheries and the whale research group at Memorial University. They have trained people who help fishermen to release whales with as little damage as possible to the gear. Many fishermen now release whales themselves.
3. Whales could be killed, either individually, when they are a threat to gear, or by resuming whaling.
4. By selling basking shark meat, fins and liver, fishermen can make money to pay for damaged gear. The local market for basking shark products is being developed.

5. Fishermen have been asking the government to give them *compensation** for damage caused by whales. This would mean the government would pay fishermen for their damaged gear. This plan would make all of us responsible for the cost of protecting whales. In 1982, there was a program of gear replacement. There were several *gear depots** around the province. At a depot, fishermen could buy sections of a codtrap to replace damaged sections. They could even buy a whole codtrap or net. This meant that the amount of lost fishing time was greatly reduced. Remember that a major problem for fishermen is the amount of time lost from fishing while gear is being repaired. By getting gear immediately from the depot, a fisherman could be fishing again much more quickly than if he must wait for the repair of damaged gear.
6. Small changes can be made in the fishing gear. Humpback whales often are trapped in the *leader* of a codtrap. (See the Gear Chart, page 77 again). The Department of Fisheries has considered what would happen if there were a slight change in the size of the leader. Would fewer whales get caught? Would the cod be affected? These questions are being studied.
7. A change in the location of codtraps may avoid some collisions. A codtrap is put in a certain location, its *berth* because there are lots of cod there. But sometimes there are lots of whales there too. Some berths seem to be more likely to be hit by whales than others. If codtraps could be located in berths where fishing is still good but whale activity is low, fewer collisions may happen. This is also being studied.
8. Fishing with trawl lines is a method that yields high quality fish that sell at a good price. Trawl lines rarely catch whales. Look again at the Gear Chart on page 77.
9. In some areas, whales are very plentiful for a short time. For example, at the peak of capelin season, whales are often numerous. It might be possible to provide the fishermen in these areas with other fishing opportunities during the times whales are there. This would create whale sanctuaries for brief periods where whales could feed but not interfere with fishermen.

Questions

13. *Do you think it is better to try to prevent collisions or to help after they happen? Why?*
14. *Can you suggest other ways in which fishermen could be helped?*

Pretend this box represents the ocean and all its resources

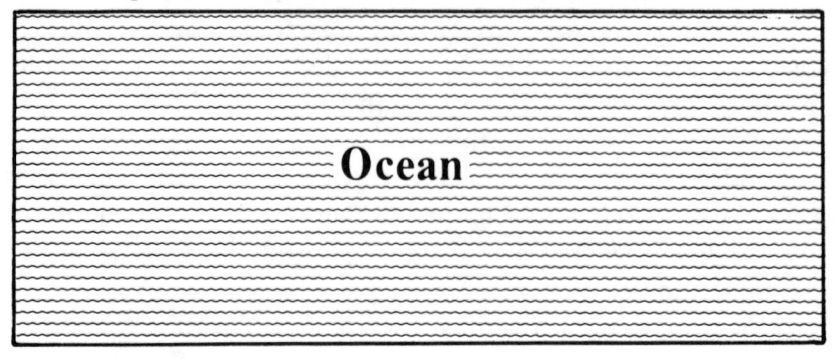

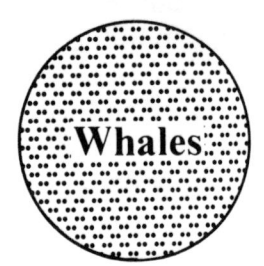

Ocean

This circle represents all the whales in the ocean and what they need and do to survive.

Whales

This circle represents humans and our use of the ocean.

Humans

We know both whales and humans use the ocean. Sometimes their activities overlap.

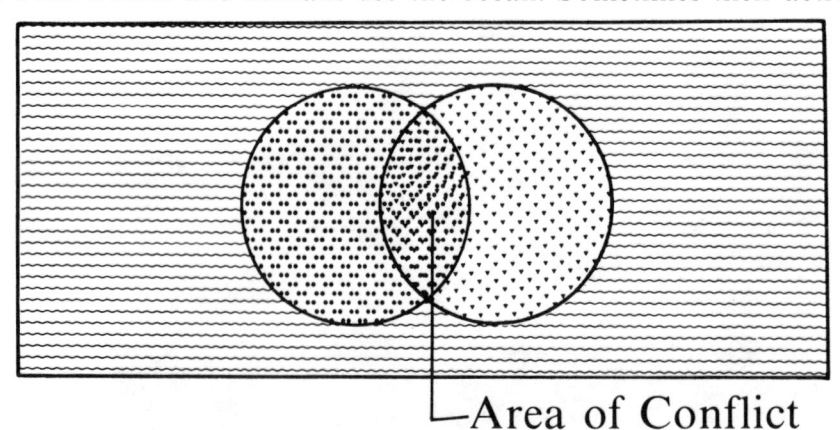

—Area of Conflict

Question

15. *Discuss some of the factors that make up the area of conflict, where the interests of whales and humans overlap.*

• **Something to Do**

1. Write the dialogue for a play in which there are three characters:
   — an 11 year old girl
   — her mother and father

   The family is gathered around the table at supper time. The father has just found a humpback in his codtrap. The whale is still alive. What do you think each one might say?
2. Write an article for a newspaper for a school in Saskatchewan. There are no whales there. **Title: A Conflict in Newfoundland - Is There a Solution?** The people who will read your article will know very little about whales and about the problem in our province. You must explain it to them.
3. Do some research! Find out about another conflict between man and a natural resource in Newfoundland and Labrador. What is the problem? What are the different sides of the problem? How is man being affected? How is the resource being affected? What are some possible solutions?
4. Do a survey of the people in your community. What do they think about the whale-fishermen conflict? Talk to fishermen. What is their opinion? You should begin by preparing a list of questions you want to ask.
5. Have a local fisherman come in and talk to the class about his experiences with whales and sharks. Be sure to ask him lots of questions. Again, you might prepare some questions in advance.

NEW WORDS

collision
   when one object or body crashes into another.

compensation
   money or goods given to make up for something lost

conflict
   a serious problem or disagreement between two opposed parties

entrapment
   when something is caught in a trap or net and cannot free itself

gear depots
   storehouses where fishing gear could be bought

CROSSWORD

Down

1. the largest type of marine mammal
2. a body of salt water, a sea
3. a battle or struggle between two groups
4. to bump into something by accident
5. types of fishing hooks used to catch cod or squid
6. if you were a cod you would not like this box
7. a kind of very large fish that gets caught up in salmon nets by accident
8. when there are no living members of a species left
9. a wooden boat used in Newfoundland

Around

13. the most easterly province in Canada
14. the people who have problems with gear damage
15. to catch by accident in a trap
16. the opposite of fighting or being in conflict with someone
    — hint: The book you are reading is a clue and the answer is two words

Across

3. food for whales and many other sea animals, a small fish that spawns inshore
10. the part of a basking shark that can be sold to make oil
11. the daily rise and fall of the ocean
12. a type of fishing gear used to catch ground fish

NEIGHBOURS

When you have completed the crossword, see what word you can make by putting the large letters together.

Getting Along — A Summary

The conflict which exists in Newfoundland and Labrador between the fishermen and whales is a very complex one. There is no easy answer. It is an example of the conflicts which exist between humans and their environment.

Humans use many of the world's natural resources, so similar conflicts are bound to develop. There are many such conflicts in Newfoundland and Labrador. Mining development in many parts of the province interfere with the migration paths of caribou herds. The timber and pulp and paper industries use the same forest resources as the province's moose populations. City developers build suburbs on land that is valuable for agriculture. You can probably think of other conflicts like this.

Problems like this have many sides. Politics and government are involved. Money and economics must be considered. The social and cultural viewpoints are important. Finally, we must pay close attention to the impact of our activities on the environment.

It is important that we are aware of these conflicts. Solutions to these problems will be found only if we are prepared to try to understand all sides of the issues. Only by gaining the cooperation of the people who use a resource, the government and researchers studying the problem, can we learn more about what makes up these conflicts and find good solutions.

To use any of our natural resources wisely, and make certain they will always be available, we need to educate ourselves about our environment. It is a two-way street. We need to know about the impact natural resources have on our lives, as well as how *our* way of life affects the world around us.

The ocean has always been very important to Newfoundland and Labrador. Its resources supply us with food, transportation, minerals, energy and recreation. Humans and whales both play important roles in the ocean environment. There is plenty of room for us both to use its vast resources cooperatively and wisely. We must learn to get along.

Printed in Canada

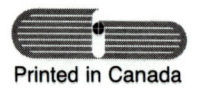